CW01510582

STAGES

AN AUTOBIOGRAPHY

STAGES

AN AUTOBIOGRAPHY

JAY OSMOND

with Kandilyn Osmond and Terri Shoemaker

Sourced Media Books
San Clemente, CA

Sourced Media Books
20 Via Cristobal
San Clemente, CA 92673
www.sourcedmediabooks.com

ISBN-13: 978-0-9841068-4-4

Printed in the United States of America.

This publication is designed to provide entertainment value and
is sold with the understanding that the publisher is not engaged
in rendering legal, accounting, or other professional advice of any
kind. If legal advice or other expert assistance is required, the ser-
vices of a competent professional person should be sought.

—From a Declaration of Principles jointly adopted by a
Committee of the American Bar Association and a
Committee of Publishers and Associations

This book is dedicated to my parents,
George & Olive Osmond

As Marie so wonderfully puts it, "I had the greatest stage
parents. They were there for me at every stage of my life."

CONTENTS

ACKNOWLEDGMENTS

This book has finally come to fruition thanks to my friend and personal assistant, Terri Shoemaker. She jokingly encouraged me for at least ten years to get my stories down on paper. She began by helping me collect pictures and putting together thoughts that were important to me. She then convinced me that I needed to start my own website (jayosmond.com) and keep our friends and fans updated. She has an amazing talent for writing and an innate ability to know what readers want.

Because of the overwhelming response to the website, we felt it was time to write my story. I wanted to share personal memories, lessons learned, and some of my favorite photos from my personal collection.

My wife, Kandilyn, also played a big part in helping me put this project together. She has a wit and a writing style that enabled me to better communicate my thoughts. I also want to thank her for the countless hours she spent sorting through hundreds of boxes of my personal memorabilia, photos, and favorite quotes that were selected for this book.

Another person I must thank is my son Jason. While on a mission for The Church of Jesus Christ of Latter-day Saints, he challenged me to be committed to this project. He inspired me to not only meet this goal, but to have it completed before he returned in two years.

I'm also grateful to my niece, Amy Osmond Cook (Wayne and Kathy's daughter), and Sourced Media Books for publishing this book. Amy has been a motivating force in our family her whole life and was excited to help me publish my story.

While writing this book, I reflected back on so many other special people not in this book that have come and gone throughout the various stages of my life, such as Karl Engemann, who did so many wonderful things for our family over the years; Allen Finlinson, one funny guy, a fantastic road manager, and a great friend to our family; Nick Gasdik, a true character, great guy, and good sport when he came along with Donny and me in England; Genelle Larsen, who co-wrote an unpublished book with me in the early 1980s about the importance of reading the scriptures; Ed Greene, a wonderful engineer and friend; Michael Lloyd, a great producer and friend; band members from over the years (Denny Crockett, Ike Egan, Sam Foster, Rich Dixon, Jimmy Bruno, Judd Maher, Kenny Hodges, Warren Trulson, Rick Baptist, Walt Johnson, Craig Turley, Bryan Hofheins, Whit Privette, Mike McAdoo, Ken Michaelis, Myles Mylenbush, Jay Brandon, Casey Smith, George Mason, Tami Art, Babette Young, Bryan Lawson, Steve Mason, Gene Puckett, Scott Taylor, Aaron Smith, and David Osmond); Bo Donaldson and The Heywoods, one of our opening acts in the 1970s; Patti Roman, a trusted friend to the whole family; Cathy Kinsella, who has tirelessly assisted our family over the years; Rob Dias, a longtime friend; Jackie Skinner, a wonderful person who continues to be a great help and devoted friend to the whole family; Gwen Taylor, who was so helpful to me when I learned the world of real estate; Lorraine Wheeler, Bev Looker, Bev Bowerman, and Judy Taylor, who have helped me so much over the years; and so many other wonderful people I have crossed paths with.

The personal photo collection of Sharon Benesta was so much help; and the wonderful photography skills of Ina Mourik for one of the book's photos and Brandon Osmond (Donny and Debbie's son) for this book's cover photos are very much appreciated.

Finally, I'd like to say thank you to my friends and family who have shared their thoughts, photos, and stories throughout these pages.

FOREWORD

What do you think it feels like to be the sixth child born into a family known across the world? Whatever it is, this feeling has been with Jay Wesley Osmond for as long as he can remember. Jay was a tender two-and-a-half years old when the family took that step into what would become stardom. For a short time, he was the baby of the family. He was the endearing little boy whose face followed the red light on the television cameras of *The Andy Williams Show.* He was the "lead" singer in a group of young brothers with inspired harmony. The journey into the world of entertainment had begun.

The children in the Osmond family were made to feel special by their parents, and each of these children is unique. They knew from the start of this journey that they each had a responsibility to be the best they could be. They did this for each other; they did it for their "fans"; and most of all they did it for our Heavenly Father. As a talent, Jay has offered superb drumming, a three-octave voice, the group's signature choreographed moves, and a keen sense of public relations. As an individual, he offers humor, compassion, support, a strong sense of faith, and a lot of love. But this only scratches the surface of this sixth child.

Jay stayed single longer than any of his siblings—and even endured some concern and criticism for that. He is the only one from the group to have actually left entertaining for a period of time and work outside the world of show business. He is also the only one of the original performing Osmonds to pursue a college degree. Having been out there in the world, without the entertainment persona to accompany him, in many ways Jay has experienced life differently than his siblings.

When you meet Jay Osmond, you feel like you've known him for years. When he becomes your friend, you know you have a true friend. Jay is a patient man, a helper, a fixer, a "guardian angel" here on earth. He often becomes so concerned with helping others that he creates his own chaos. I've never seen a more disorganized person with the desire to be orderly and efficient in my life. However, he is amazing at remembering details that have long since tumbled to the back of most people's minds. He remembers faces and names. He remembers dates, knows what places looked like, and recalls the circumstances around different events. With his ability to remember so precisely, it is fascinating to hear Jay recount his life's experiences and the valuable lessons he's learned during each stage of his life thus far. I knew that with more than 50 years of seeing the world, performing countless concerts, and meeting people from all walks of life, Jay had a story to tell.

It took a little prodding on my part to get Jay to seriously commit to this project. He wanted to tell his story but was a bit overwhelmed with how to start. It took at least two years to get everything onto paper, and I think writing this book about Jay's life ended up being a journey in itself. Because Jay has been on stage for most of his life (and he knew he wanted to call his book *Stages*), I had the idea to present the book as though it were a script for a play. Jay, Kandi, and I came up with the outline based on his life in five-year increments, and then I began asking Jay a series of questions about each time frame. We took his responses and formed them into stories. Once Jay went through those stories, it was as though a floodgate opened. Stories came spilling out of him, and I became increasingly glad he decided to write this book.

I was amazed by the connection Jay still has with the friends who contributed to this book. Even if they hadn't been in touch for a while, it was as though their friendship never missed a beat (no pun intended). To me, that is the sign of true friendship.

This book has been a part of my life for so long, the completion almost felt like saying goodbye to an old friend. I can't thank Jay enough for trusting me to be a part of this very special project. Yes, it has been quite a journey writing this book with Jay and Kandi. It has involved a lot of hours, organization, research, writing and rewriting . . . and I wouldn't have traded a moment of it.

Jay, the sixth child of the Osmond family, is a kind soul, a caring individual, a wonderful family man, and a tremendous talent. He is special to each of the Osmonds in so many ways. When his siblings were asked to define Jay in one word, their responses were: Counselor (Virl), Considerate (Tom), Positive (Alan), Thoughtful (Wayne), Genuine (Merrill), Kind (Donny), Caring (Marie), and Awesome (Jimmy). These eight words speak volumes about Jay Osmond, and I am honored to call him "friend."

I hope you enjoy Jay Osmond's *Stages: An Autobiography.*

—*Terri Shoemaker*

Introduction

SETTING THE STAGE

MY MISSION

The purpose of the Osmond family is to lighten the load of others by bringing music that carries with it a message of hope—that life can be enjoyed and lived with an abundance of love. That is our message. That is our dream.

My mission is to be a part of this family, whose ministry is to help bring souls to Christ. That's what it is all about, no matter what stage of life we are in. We are all children of God, and He loves us the same—no matter what we've done or what our station in life is. He always has His arms open to us.

Helping others to find the Gospel is what brings me joy and happiness. Even if we bring one soul to Christ, our mission will be complete.

Every stage of my life has helped me to build faith in Jesus Christ and in His Gospel.

MY LIFE IS AN OPEN BOOK

If you've been around since the 1960s and 70s, maybe you've heard of my family, The Osmonds. My name is Jay Wesley Osmond, and I am the sixth of nine children. I have been performing with my family since I was two-and-a-half years old. Together we've had a great run of over 50 years in the crazy world of show business. We've had number one hits and numerous gold and platinum records; we've performed for Presidents of the United States and the Queen of England; and we've had successful runs headlining in major venues throughout the world. One of our record albums was taken to the moon by Neil Armstrong; and when they played the song, "Aquarius," on the moon, it was the rendition with the Osmond Brothers singing backup for Andy Williams. We've been honored with many awards including a star on The Hollywood Walk of Fame; and we have have had sell-out tours, produced top-rated television shows, performed with many celebrities, and had several documentaries produced about our family. We have also experienced many ups and downs and have been blessed with success and failure. We've had a lot of children collectively and have experienced many heartaches and triumphs, individually.

Due to the constant spotlight I have lived under, I sometimes feel like my life has been an open book, as though I have lived on a stage all of my life. Those feelings are what led me to write this book about my life as though it has been a series of scenes in a play. This book contains my version of stories as I remember them happening (my brothers and sister may have different versions from their recollections). I hope you enjoy it.

Sincerely,

Jay Osmond

Act 1

~1955—1960~

OGDEN ROOTS

WORK AND PLAY

When Family Night was introduced by The Church of Jesus Christ of Latter-day Saints to its members in the late 1950s, my parents loved the idea. It was in our living room in Ogden, Utah, where we started having Family Night consistently once a week. My parents came up with many interesting activities, and our weekly meetings always involved a religious lesson, games, and music. One of the things we always included was singing. My father used to be in a choir and loved to sing. Probably as much as he loved singing, my sweet little mother loved to listen to him while she would accompany him on the piano. She would also sing beautifully off-key, though it didn't matter—we loved her voice. We were encouraged to harmonize with each other, because we seemed to have a natural talent in this area and our family enjoyed listening to us. It became a tradition to learn a new song each week for Family Night.

Our oldest brothers, Virl and Tom (whom I have always viewed as the heroes of our family), were born with hearing impairments. My mother came up with the idea to have them learn to play the saxophone instead of singing (she loved that instrument and played it in a dance band when she was younger). They also tried to teach sign language to us—of which we managed to learn a little. Most importantly, Virl and Tom taught me to hear with my heart. I have always used Virl and Tom as my examples when things were tough. I'd say to myself, "If they can do it, so can I."

Alan, Wayne, Merrill, and I formed a barbershop quartet and called ourselves "The Osmond Brothers." We became known around town and were soon being asked to sing at church and civic events, as well as local birthday parties. A vocal teacher by the name of Val Hicks heard us sing one night and told us we had tremendous talent. He wanted to help us further improve our skills and knew of some companies that he was sure would hire us to sing. My father thought having Val coach us was a good idea and asked us if we wanted to do it. I was so young that I just went along with everything my brothers did. My brother Alan thought we could get jobs singing and make money to buy better hearing aids for Virl and Tom, and my mother thought we could also contribute some money to the mission fund she started for all of us to use someday.

At the time, none of us imagined that our little singing quartet would go any further than those original goals. I believe our Family Nights helped us to learn more about our religion, develop our talents, and create a bond that kept us strong as a family. I also think it was because of that bond that we were able to enter the world of entertainment and enjoy success while we remained grounded in our beliefs.

Many happy days were spent in the backyard and farm area of our home in Ogden, Utah. Wayne used to hide his cap guns from me, but I always found them and shot them when he wasn't looking. My brothers and I used to build things like airplanes made out of wood, or we constructed trains by hooking up wagons.

I love those memories from what I now see as a simpler time, though things didn't always feel simple back then. I experienced challenges and learned lessons from them just like any other kid. I remember being threatened a lot by a weird teenager after school as I walked by the Waynesguard Food Store. He just didn't like me. I would bravely walk home from kindergarten and try to deal with his bullying. I finally had the courage to tell my parents and my teacher about this kid. I turned the situation around by telling him I did so. I learned to take that fear, face it, and confront it. So I'm thankful to that "bully" all those years ago, who presented me with one of my first opportunities to conquer fear.

There was also the learning experience I had resulting from a particular trip to the store with my mother at about age five. I wanted a piece of candy so badly. My mother said "no," but I took a piece, anyway, and hid it in my pocket. I felt so bad afterwards and felt too guilty to eat it, so I gave it to my brother Merrill. I learned about honesty that day and the importance of exercising patience in waiting for things. I discovered I had a conscience at that early age. I've always wished I would have told my mother at the time, because I now know she would have simply made me pay for the candy and given me a hug.

Another lesson I learned during this stage of my life is how the comfort of home can be challenged in the blink of an eye. Our house was behind a juvenile detention center, and there were a few occasions (and they were pretty eerie) when several of those juveniles broke out of the center and ran through our yard. They would bang on our doors and run and scream loudly, and it was very frightening for me as a small child. I had mixed feelings about growing up near this center but learned that the world isn't always a safe place, no matter where you are. It taught me that I never wanted to live life being afraid. It really made me appreciate my safe and secure home life, and I felt sad for those children who didn't have that. I knew that someday, when I had my own family, it would be important to me that they felt safe. My parents taught us that you can't always protect your children from the world, but you can insulate them. I believe this to be true.

Several fond memories stand out in my mind from the years we lived in Ogden. I remember seeing one of Santa's reindeer in my window above my bed. Christmastime was magical to our family. Another memory is how my brother Alan blew his trumpet to wake us up for revelry every morning. Our father used to be an Army sergeant, and his ways of discipline infiltrated our lifestyle, which included him building a dormitory for my brothers and me.

I remember flirting at age five with Cathy, the girl who lived across the fence from us. I thought that little girl was the "cat's meow." There were many times when we gathered as a family in front of our old black-and-white television and watched *The Andy Williams Show*. Little did we know what an important role Andy Williams would play in our lives.

We had a Golden Retriever that I loved named "Tip." I was emotionally very lonely as a kid. Even though we were a close family, I needed a special connection that only my dogs could fill. Even though my mother didn't like pets, she allowed me to have my dogs.

Because I have so many wonderful memories from our days in Ogden, there was a time I felt angry we left it. Our home was a wonderful place—and sadly, in 1999 it was torn down. I felt depressed about this move toward "progress," but I've come to learn that when you go back and try to relive something as you remember it, it is never the same. Today a Lowe's Home Improvement Store sits on the property where our home once stood. If you ever find yourself in Ogden, Utah on Washington Blvd., think of me when you walk into the store—the front entrance is where our living room used to be.

THE LIVING ROOM

One of my fondest memories from those early days in Ogden is the sandbox that was just to the south side of the house. This is where I spent a lot of my time playing with trucks and toy farm animals. At age four, I remember not being very happy when my father would call me to the living room to practice singing with my brothers.

I hated when my world of creativity was interrupted for singing practice, and we practiced every day. My father taught us that if we were going to be singers, it was not only important to be good—we had to be the best. There was not a day I can remember when we didn't include singing in our life back then. We'd stand around the organ in our living room, and sing, sing, sing. (I sometimes felt like I was in the prison, "Sing Sing!")

I think my brothers and sister also felt, to a degree, that we were pushed too hard as young kids to practice our music. In later years, our father expressed regret that he may have been too hard on us. However, we learned the importance of hard work. Each of us had chores that we were expected to do in addition to singing. I actually looked at my chores as a welcomed break from singing. I do feel too much was put on me too soon, and I have since come to believe that balance is the key to everything we do in life.

I don't think we could have accomplished the things we have without a strong father and mother who loved and guided us. We always worked hard, but we played hard, too.

I went through some rough times but later realized so many blessings resulted from the sacrifices we made. In looking back on these experiences, and the efforts we made, I know all of it contributed to our long careers in the entertainment industry. It really all started in our living room. A place I once considered a prison is now a place I treasure in my memories.

THE LIFESTYLE

Our lifestyle was very structured and organized. It had to be. There were eight children at the time, Donny and Marie being the youngest. We lived on a farm, and my parents operated a couple of businesses. In addition, Alan, Wayne, Merrill, and I were working as a singing group. Virl and Tom attended a school for the deaf and were also involved in Boy Scouts. That's not to mention we were all active in our church. They were hard but happy times. One of the things I learned through all of our activities is that busy is better.

Our father supervised the post office at Five Points (a street in Ogden), and he was also an agent at Safeco Insurance. I remember many times helping to sort the mail at the post office, which was adjacent to Grandpa and Grandma Davis's house. My grandma's brother John had an apartment that was connected to their home. I never saw my Uncle John when he wasn't drunk.

Our grandparents, Tom and Vera Davis, were an integral part of our family in those early days. We used to go over to their house a lot, and Grandpa would take us to the A&W store and buy ice cream cones. He would put me on his chest as he sat back in his big chair and whistle. Grandma Davis was fussing all the time, trying to cook something special for us.

We were uncomfortable going over to Grandma Osmond's house for some reason. I think it was because she was stern and orderly to an obsessive degree. She had a little dog named "Mickey." Mickey was an irritating little Chihuahua with a yippy bark, and he would always nip at me. As I grew older, my perception changed about both Grandma Osmond and little Mickey. I gained a real respect for Grandma Osmond and saw her in a different light, as a woman full of wisdom. I even learned to like that dang little Chihuahua.

Along with our parents, each of us had a job or two. My jobs consisted of taking out the garbage, drying the dishes, and cleaning up the backyard. (Come to think of it, those are still my jobs!)

We made countless appearances in Salt Lake City and neighboring areas. It seemed we were always getting into the car to go and perform a show somewhere. I remember a time when my father was speeding and was pulled over by a police officer. The officer asked why we were all dressed alike, and my father said we were a group and were late for our performance. Father proceeded to ask the officer if he would like to hear us sing. The police officer couldn't really turn down an offer like that; and after we sang "Side By Side" to him, he let us go with a warning. That was exactly what my father had hoped he would do. My father could talk anyone into (or out of) anything.

I will never forget the very first time we got paid for singing. That first show was for the Wheeler Machinery Company in Salt Lake City. I was still in diapers and couldn't believe people were throwing money at me. As I was picking up the coins, my brothers tried to keep the song going through the laughter of the audience. I knew from that time on, we were not the average family.

Along with everything else I was doing, I went to kindergarten at Lincoln Elementary School in Ogden. I made many friends at school, such as Cathy (the girl next door), and Katrina, whom I considered to be my "girlfriend." I also had a crush on my kindergarten teacher, Mrs. Bethority, who was a great teacher. One time she had the class work on an art project that was so exciting, I didn't want anything to interrupt it, not even for "nature's call." I was so embarrassed when I didn't make it to the bathroom in time, but Mrs. Bethority saved the day (and what was left of my dignity) by letting me go home to change my pants.

Life was good in Ogden. My first grade teacher, Mrs. Morse, was my next door neighbor. I felt bad that Mr. and Mrs. Morse were depicted as annoying neighbors in *Side By Side*, the movie about our parents' life. As portrayed in the movie, they did tease us about all the laundry we always had hanging to dry in our backyard, but they were wonderful people and my parents loved them.

The movie was a little sugar-coated (as my family saw it), but I wanted to show how Mother saw life back then. I was the executive producer for the movie, and Mother was the consultant. Marie played the role of our mother. We worked very hard each day and night to make sure Mother's input was in the movie and that our life in Ogden was carefully documented the way she remembered it. I even allowed the writers to keep the line in the script that had the little actor who portrayed me say, "We don't want to work—we want to sing." That wasn't exactly how I felt, but I knew my mother thought that line in the script was cute, so I left it in. (By the way, the organ used in the movie was the original from our living room.)

DISNEYLAND

Our first television appearance was on *The Eugene Gelesnik Show* on KSL Television. I was five years old, and it didn't really register with me that I was actually on television. Grandpa Davis bought a clip from that show and sent it to *The Lawrence Welk Show* in hopes of getting us an audition. I was about six years old when we drove all the way from Utah to audition for Lawrence Welk in California. We waited several hours for him to see us, only to have his assistant finally tell us he was too busy (and apologized for the imposition). Our father was upset but said we were not going to make the trip to California fruitless, so we jumped into the car and headed for Disneyland. Because we were all dressed alike from the cancelled audition for Lawrence Welk, we stood out in the crowd, especially to the barbershop group, The Dapper Dans. They were a singing group that performed on the streets of Disneyland. They asked us if we were a singing group, and we told them yes—we were! We sang one song for them, and then another. They sang to us, and we sang for them again as a crowd gathered in the street. It was quite a commotion. The Dapper Dans were so impressed that they took us to meet their boss, Tommy Walker. Mr. Walker seemed impressed with our singing, as well, and told us he would be in touch.

Jim Lennon, a boxing announcer and uncle of The Lennon Sisters, felt bad that we didn't get our audition with Lawrence Welk, so he invited us to sing during half time at a boxing match the next day. The response was less than favorable. We left that performance having learned that an audience at a boxing match wasn't very interested in listening to a barbershop quartet made up of four little boys.

After we returned home to Utah, we received a call from Tommy Walker. He wanted us to travel back to Orange County and audition for Walt Disney. I couldn't believe it. That trip was a long way in a car for a little kid, but back to California we went. We met Walt Disney and performed the song, "Side By Side," for him. Wow, what a moment! I was so excited that we were singing for the guy who invented Mickey Mouse.

Walt Disney struck me as a nervous type of person who laughed a lot and was always smoking. I'll never forget when he sat me on his lap and drew a picture of Mickey Mouse for me. He signed the drawing, "To my buddy Jay, Love, Walt Disney." (I wish I still had that picture he drew for me.) I couldn't believe all of this was happening.

Walt Disney loved our singing and had us learn the song, "I Want a Girl." The routine he taught us included some choreographed movements with hats and mustaches. I completely messed up the routine, but it really made Mr. Disney laugh—and he insisted we keep the mistakes in. In fact, Mr. Disney had The Dapper Dans include the song and routine in their show. It was fun later on in life to perform "I Want a Girl" with Bob Hope on one of our TV specials. Bob Hope played my part, and I had the pleasure of teaching him how to mess up the routine.

All of our hard work was finally starting to develop into something. Our audition with Walt Disney resulted in us being put on four Disney television shows. A wonderful window of opportunity was opening up for us despite not being able to audition for Lawrence Welk . . . and our lives were never going to be the same. It was quite a concept for me to learn that we could make mistakes (like I did in the "I Want a Girl" routine) and that it would not only be all right, but it would also become a part of our act. That concept would change, however, when we joined *The Andy Williams Show.*

Many years later, we performed on Disney's 25th Anniversary television special. I recall us performing in front of the riverboat in Disneyland and reflecting back on our start at this very park. I marveled at the fact that we were part of Disney's 25th Anniversary celebration and wondered if our own group could make it to such a milestone. When we did reach our own 25th Anniversary in show business, I realized it might be possible that we'd someday be celebrating our "golden anniversary." We've surpassed that anniversary, as well. As the old adage goes, "Time flies when you're having fun."

Act 2

~1961—1965~

CALIFORNIA DREAMING

ANDY WILLIAMS

Our exposure on the Disney television shows (in the series, *Disneyland After Dark*) led to Andy Williams' father, Jay Williams, "discovering" us. He was quite impressed with our singing and suggested to his son, Andy (who had a very popular television show at the time), that he should seriously consider listening to us.

I really didn't understand what was happening to my life at the time but realized people really liked our group. I remember thinking, during our audition for Andy, that this big star I'd watched on television was now looking me straight in the eyes. He seemed to like us, and the four of us found ourselves surrounded by television cameras the very next week as we sang, "Be My Little Baby Bumble Bee." It was 1962, and I was six years old, Merrill was eight, Wayne was ten, and Alan was twelve. Before the show, the director told us there would be four cameras working simultaneously. He explained that the camera with the red light turned on would be the one that millions of people would be looking at us through. The idea of this scared me a lot, but being anxious to do a good job, I was determined to get it right. As we entered the stage and started singing, the cameras surrounded us, so I began to look for the one with the red light turned on. They would switch back and forth from camera to camera, and my eyes and head would follow. My brothers were focused straight ahead throughout the number, as we were supposed to be doing, but I thought I was doing the right thing—not them. Apparently this was very funny and the audience began to laugh. When I realized what was happening and saw the reaction I was getting from the audience, I started to like the idea of all that attention—so I continued looking for the red light.

The television audience seemed to love us, and we were told that thousands of letters arrived at NBC referring to my watching the camera. At first it was a little bit of an ego trip; I realized people were finding my following the cameras cute and humorous, so I continued to look for the camera's red light to keep it funny. In doing so, that pressure soon caused me to start to lose the desire to want to be in the spotlight. However, when our brother Donny joined the group a year later, I felt a little jealous of all the attention he was getting. I was torn with my feelings at the time but laugh when I look back at it now.

I have a lot of good memories from those Andy Williams appearances and a few bad ones, as well. My brothers and I had the heavy burden for the next seven years of rigorous rehearsals and the pressure to get our songs and choreography perfect. We persevered and became known as the "One-take Osmonds." Before the final taping each Friday, we would sit in our dressing room with the lights out and focus on what was about to take place. This experience was horrifying, to say the least. What got me through the hard times was a bond with my brothers, the love and guidance of our parents, and prayer. We had family prayer every day, and I spent a lot of time in personal prayer, as well. It got me through the fear, the anxiety, and the pressure I felt performing on national television at a very young age.

The people we worked with on that show were great but very demanding. Andy Williams was always very nice, though somewhat distant. To this day, I have a great respect for him as a professional. I watched and learned how he handled things with class and dignity, as he was always cool under fire.

Among the things we had to quickly put into our act while on the show were ice skating, pianos, tumbling, juggling, instruments, and tough dance routines. Every week we felt we had to be perfect, because we had to live up to the image of the "One-take Osmonds." It was that kind of thinking that took my brothers and me down mentally in later years. Just the thought of doing things in one take really brought back haunting memories for all of us. If we could go back, the only thing I would want to change would be the one-take mentality.

CALIFORNIA, HERE WE COME!

By the time we finished the first season of *The Andy Williams Show*, we were anxious to get back home to Utah. I was in second grade at the time and was enrolled in the Los Angeles school system. We would go back and forth from California to Utah to do the show every few weeks. With all of the traveling back and forth, I really began to see our family as "different." I especially became aware of this when we made a permanent move to California. We were always being pulled out of the public school system when we worked and traveled. During those times, we hired private tutors and tried to keep up with our assignments. I realized this was very different from how other kids were living. My mother was very worried about this and wanted us to be as "normal" as possible. We all wanted that, too. I think it was that desire that helped to keep us from getting off-track in show business.

I could tell from an early age that my mother was very concerned about keeping us grounded. She knew that we were involved in an unusual whirlwind but also sensed there was a higher purpose to all of this. My mother tried every way possible to instruct us in the basics of education as well as to keep us balanced spiritually at home. She taught us that the most important learning takes place in the home. She also believed that learning in every arena, not just in the classroom, was a goal for us all to remember.

During the off-season, our manager, Don Williams (Andy Williams's brother) brought a script to us from MGM studios called *The Travels of Jaimie McPheeters.* It had the four of us brothers playing the parts of the Kissel Brothers. The executives at MGM thought we would be just right for this television series, which ran from 1963–65.

It was a wonderful experience and a great diversion for my brothers and me as we played a family of pioneers who traveled by wagon train out West. We sang and acted in this series. Kurt Russell played the part of Jaimie McPheeters and was a great help to us with acting tips. I was amazed at Kurt's acting ability. I remember one time Kurt was telling us a funny story, and we were all laughing so hard. Suddenly the director yelled, "Action!" Kurt immediately stopped laughing and went into character. I continued to laugh and got into a bit of trouble. This was a real learning experience for me. Kurt became almost like a brother to us during this time frame.

In 1964, we received another acting opportunity. The offer was for a movie, *Bob Hope Presents the Seven Little Foys,* and was based on the true story of vaudeville performer, Eddie Foy, a widowed father and his seven children who performed with him. I was honored to play the part of Eddie Foy, Jr. The real Eddie Foy, Jr. played the part of his father, Eddie Foy. My brothers and I were able to relate so well to the situations this family had to go through working in show business. In addition to meeting Eddie Foy, Jr., we had the opportunity to work with Bob Hope, who was the host of this program, and Mickey Rooney, who played the role of George M. Cohan.

Bob Hope really had a deep love for our family, and we loved him, too. He later became the "Honorary President" of The Children's Miracle Network. This charity (started by my parents) was originally formed to help children with hearing impairments but later expanded to help all causes for children. As of 2010, The

Children's Miracle Network has raised more than 3.4 billion dollars for children. I know this has pleased my parents and our family very much.

A WORLD OF ENTERTAINERS

One of the exciting aspects of being in entertainment is meeting other people in the business. We met and worked with so many entertainers, it is hard to say who made the biggest impact on me.

Most of them, to me, seemed to be just "ordinary people," though sometimes a bit eccentric. I guess a little eccentricity has to be involved to even want to be in this business. When we were on *The Andy Williams Show* and *The Jerry Lewis Show,* it seemed normal to meet and talk with at least two or three celebrities each week.

It is amazing to me how all of us have within ourselves a desire to be recognized and feel important. I have found that many people in the entertainment industry are a little insecure and feel a need to be associated with other entertainers in order to relate and not feel alone. The only thing that bothers me about this is the act of "name dropping." In fact, one day, I remember Frank Sinatra and I were talking about this very topic!

We missed out on an exciting opportunity early on—around 1964, when we performed with the Brooks Sisters at the Texas State Fair. We had a day off, and the Brooks Sisters were going to see a group called The Beatles. Their agent knew some of the people who were involved in putting together The Beatles' American tour, and they invited us to see the show with them. Instead, we decided to just take the day off and go to the fair. The Brooks Sisters went to the concert without us and returned with a picture of The Beatles, signed, "To the Osmond Brothers, Sorry we missed you! —John Lennon." To this day, I regret not keeping that picture.

Lucille Ball was really interesting. We visited Lucille at her home sometime in the mid-1970s. Her children and a few other friends were there. She threw a big party for us. We played all day in her pool and had a great time. She really went out of her way to be sure we laughed and had fun. Lucille Ball was a very opinionated person, sometimes in an almost domineering way. She was a little rough around the edges but very sweet and sensitive inside. You could tell she'd had a lot of hurt in her life.

I remember a near disaster I experienced on *The Andy Williams Show*. I was about seven or eight years old at the time. We had a production number every week, which usually involved a guest artist. This particular week, our production number was with Julie Andrews, who was promoting her movie, *Mary Poppins*. We were honored to perform the song, "Supercalifragilisticexpialidocious," with her. I found the idea of working with Julie Andrews, along with my fascination for the movie, enthralling. I even lost a sense of reality to the point where I got on the roof of our home and honestly thought I could jump off with an umbrella and float down. I'm glad my father saw me and ordered me down. It was clear that my life evolved around show business and the magical life we were living; it was almost like we weren't living in reality full-time. For a young kid like me with a big imagination, it was hard to see celebrities on television and not be a little confused when I saw them in normal situations. When we went to our summer home in Huntsville, it was always an adjustment to get back to normal life.

I met John Wayne during the late 1960s when he was a guest on *The Jerry Lewis Variety Hour*. We were working with Jerry regularly on his show and met a lot of celebrities each week.

I couldn't believe I actually met John Wayne. He was very nice to us and was very dignified, but he seemed to be in a lot of pain. We later learned he was suffering from cancer. Looking ahead a few years, I remember him taking the time to put his handprints and signature in a block of cement to be put on the Star Wall (along with other celebrities) outside our television studio in Orem, Utah. He had to do it for us three times, because each time we displayed his handprints on the "Star Wall," the block would be stolen. The third time he did it, he punched the cement instead of imprinting his hands. That imprint was also stolen.

Margaret Hamilton is another celebrity who impressed me. I met her at the ABC studios in Hollywood when we were both appearing as guests on *The ABC Chevrolet Special.* Being a big fan of the classic movie, *The Wizard of Oz,* I couldn't pass up the opportunity to meet her. I walked over to her, introduced myself, and told her she scared the heck out of me as a child. Her response of laughter was a weird déjà vu moment for me. I just couldn't make the connection in my mind between this sweet little lady and the Wicked Witch. She told me how she loved to tell her grandkids stories about the making of the movie, and how they liked to invite their friends over to see her while they watched it. She said she was actually sick of watching the movie so many times. Meeting Margaret Hamilton and talking with her really was a thrill for me.

Another déjà vu moment came for me later in my life when I met Barbara Eden. I told her I used to be her biggest fan when she was on the *I Dream of Jeannie* television show. Barbara replied, "Used to?" We laughed and talked, and the whole while I couldn't believe it was really her. At a Los Angeles autograph convention I attended with Wayne and Merrill in February 2010, I saw so many people whom I'd either met in the past or had always wanted to meet when I was a kid. It was fun to be part of such a great event. One of the best parts was visiting a booth where they were selling "genie bottles" featuring the person who designed the bottle for *I Dream of Jeannie.* I got one of the bottles for Kandi for Valentine's Day and shortly after ran into Larry Hagman (who was also taking part in the convention). We worked with Larry many years ago on *The Jerry Lewis Show*, and it was great to see him again. He was being whisked away for an interview, but I really wanted to take advantage of the rare opportunity to have him autograph the bottle for Kandi. I hurried over to him, and he stopped to say hello. He was so gracious to take the time to sign the bottle. I have found that most entertainers are really very wonderful people.

Jane Russell is a wonderful celebrity whom I also met at that autograph convention. I walked over to her booth and gave her a picture of me and my brothers. She looked at the photo and said, "Wow, for me? Thank you!" The photographers started snapping photos of us, and Ms. Russell turned to me and said, "Don't forget to say cheese!" She reminded me so much of my wife's sweet little grandmother, Rose, and I gave her a little kiss on the head. Then, I looked down at the table where she was signing autographs and "hot babe" photos once taken of her—and that really freaked me out!

Cher made quite an impression on me. My brothers and I were guests on *The Sonny and Cher Show* around 1976. This was right around the time we made our first television special with George Burns and Isaac Hayes. It was also about the same time we made appearances on *The Flip Wilson Show, The Mac Davis Show,* and *The Glen Campbell Goodtime Hour.* I choreographed a Stevie Wonder number for Cher to do with my brothers and me. Looking back, this was a lot of pressure for me, but Cher reminded me so much of my sister, Marie. Cher made me feel important and treated me with a lot of respect. This was the first time I felt like I was really in charge of something, and the experience prepared me for when I would work on *The Donny and Marie Show*, as well as the *Marie* specials and the movie about our family, *Side By Side*.

In 1973, our family was performing in Paris, and we stayed at the George IV Hotel. We found out that Paul McCartney was staying at the same hotel, so we asked the manager if it could be arranged for us to meet him. He said he didn't think so because Paul was about to leave but said he would check for us. About an hour later we received a call in our suite. If I remember correctly, it was Alan who answered the phone and discovered it was Paul McCartney on the other end of the line. Paul asked if it would be all right to visit our suite with his wife, Linda, and their two daughters, Heather and Mary. He said that the girls would like to get an autograph. We were astounded to think that our idol would be that humble, and we couldn't believe he was asking for *our* autographs. They were all such nice people, and it is a night we remember well.

Glenn Beck is another person that stands out in my mind. I met him in Florida at a convention for The Children's Miracle Network. Glenn was preparing to give a speech, and I could tell he was under stress; however, he went out of his way and took time to meet me and my family. Whether or not you believe in Glenn Beck's political theories, I think he is to be admired and respected —he's a great individual.

Andy Williams once said he never took many opportunities to get to know all of the celebrities he'd worked with on his television show, and I have that same regret. There have been so many wonderful people in show business that I didn't take the time to get to know. I think that is why I later took the time with celebrities like Jaclyn Smith (I admit I had an ulterior motive), Olivia Newton-John, Debbie Reynolds, David Hasselhoff, Tony Geary, Herb Alpert, Bob Hope, Ann-Margret, Andy Gibb, and others. I showed them around Utah when they came to the Osmond Studios to guest star on our show.

Like the rest of the world, I was greatly saddened by the passing in 2009 of Michael Jackson. I met Michael in 1972 and found him to be a compelling and amazingly talented person.

The Osmonds were performing at the CNE (Canadian National Exposition) in Toronto, Canada, and the Jacksons were scheduled to perform the following day. The Jacksons were staying at the same hotel. We had a great time getting together with their family and had a fun night playing football in the hallways and ordering a ton of food. I remember Michael calling me a "turkey" in fun. That really caught me by surprise, because no one had called me a "turkey" before. (Sometimes now, when I'm having fun with my sons, I'll call them "turkeys," and it always reminds me of that time.) Michael told me he was once asked by a reporter how he felt about the press comparing the Jackson 5 to the Osmonds. Michael's response to the question was, "We're as different as night and day!" I thought that was really funny. Michael had a unique sense of humor.

The Jackson family said when they were kids, their father made them sit around the television and watch the Osmond Brothers perform on *The Andy Williams Show*. Our families had many similarities, including our mothers having the same birthday. We shared many experiences, having both come into the pop scene in the 1970s, and understood the internal pressures of how hard it is to live a normal life in show business. Sadly, Michael never seemed to find a balance to ease that constant pressure.

Also in the 1970s, while in England at Earl's Court (a large arena in London), we were honored when Led Zeppelin invited us on stage to sing "Stairway to Heaven" with them. It was a surreal moment for me as I played congas next to John Bonham. John later showed me his Rolls Royce, which made me want to get one. I eventually did—a gold and green one.

Some of the celebrities and entertainers we've been honored to work with over the years that stand out in my mind include Kate Smith, Paul Lynde, Lee Majors, Farrah Fawcett, Vincent Price, Monty Hall, Charlton Heston, Sally Struthers, Groucho Marx, Karen Valentine, the Harlem Globetrotters, Ted Knight, The Weire Brothers, Jimmie Walker, Carl Ballantine, Ruth Buzzi, Edgar Bergen, Roy Clark, George Gobel, Charo, Raymond Burr, Esther Rolle, Peter Kastner, Sherman Hemsley, Pearl Bailey, Anne Meara, Milton Berle, Nipsey Russell, Tom Eure, Jim Nabors, Hal Linden, Ron Palillo, Robert Hegyes, Lawrence Hilton-Jacobs, Minnie Pearl, McLean Stevenson, Rick Hurst, Gabe Kaplan, Jack Albertson, The Great Tomsoni, Michael Landon, Don Knotts, Lorne Greene, Isabel Sanford, Little Richard, George Burns, Evel

Knievel, Peggy Fleming, Chubby Checker, Gale Storm, Arthur Godfrey, Alan "Elvis" Meyer, Desi Arnaz, Howdy Doody, Art Linkletter, Chad Everett, Florence Henderson, David Cassidy, The Brady Bunch, Patty Maloney, The Rice Twins, Loretta Swit, Spike Jones, Jr., Billy Barty, Sonny Bono, Cher, Cindy Williams, Charley Pride, Roz Kelly/Pinky & The Pinkettes, Roy Rogers, Dale Evans, Georgia Engel, Rich Little, Andy Griffith, Bo Diddley, Fred Berry, Muench, Haywood Nelson, Ernest Thomas, Carl Reiner, Merle Haggard, Kaptain Kool & The Kongs, Buddy Hackett, Gary Burghoff, Chuck Berry, Paul Anka, Rip Taylor, Billy Preston, Tina Turner, Connie Stevens, Keely Smith, Paul Williams, Tony Martin, Cyd Charisse, Fran Tarkenton, Ken Stabler, John Brascia, Bert Convy, Sonny James, The Silvers, Ray Bolger, Virginia Wood, Cheryl Ladd, Johnny Dark, Ben Vereen, Kristy McNichol, Billy Crystal, Big Bird, Glen Campbell, Bernadette Peters, Lucien Meyer & His Skating Chimps, Freddie Trenkler, Rod Gist, Mr. Frick, Kris Kristofferson, Redd Foxx, Rita Coolidge, Lola Falana, Don Most, Abe Vigoda, Anson Williams, Ken Berry, Mac Davis, Mackenzie Phillips, Robert Young, Neil Sadaka, Susan Perkins, Danny Thomas, Desi Arnaz, Jr., the Mormon Tabernacle Choir, Suzanne Somers, Betty White, Tom Jones, Ron Howard, Engelbert Humperdinck, Parker Stevenson, Mel Tillis, Joey Travolta, Dick Van Patten, Lassie, Robert Conrad, Lynn Hallowell, K. C. & The Sunshine Band, Maurice Gibb, several Miss Americas, Dirk Benedict, Harvey Korman, Cheryl Tieg, Gavin MacLeod, Raquel Welch, Seals & Crofts, Debby Boone, David Copperfield, The U.S. Ski Team, Leif Garrett, LeVar Burton, Joyce Dewitt, Dwight Moore's Mongrel Revue, King Arthur the Lion, Murray Hill's Elephants, Tanya Tucker, Larry Mahan, Boys Town Choir, Andrea McArdle, Adam Rich, Cathy Rigby, Wolfman Jack, Loretta Lynn, Grant Goodeve, Isaac Hayes, The Hager Twins, Tina Cole, Tony Orlando, Erik Estrada, Efrin Zimblis, Jr., the Lennon Sisters, Pat Boone, Nell Carter, The Commodores, Lionel Richie, The Pointer Sisters, Scott Baio, Ronald Reagan, Louis Armstrong, Karen Carpenter, Kenny Rogers, Oprah Winfrey, David Essex, Terry

Bradshaw, Joe Namath, E. J. Peaker, Roger Staubach, Conway Twitty, Steve Young, Shane Richie, Sergio Franchi, Bertha and Tina (performing elephants), Peter Nero, Robert Williams, Eddie Albert, Tim Conway, Sammy Davis, Jr., Steve Lawrence & Eydie Gorme, Liza Minnelli, the Dallas Cowboy Cheerleaders, Susan Anton, Danny Kaye, Bill Cosby, Ed Sullivan, Henry Mancini, Dick Clark, and many more.

Truly, we have been blessed to associate with a world of interesting and talented entertainers.

SPECIAL PLACES

I was doing quite a bit of traveling around the world at a young age and was caught between wanting to stay home in my secure spot and itching to go on all these adventures. I began to see life with a broader perspective and eventually looked at the world as one big home. As a result, I started to develop a need for special places that left a good feeling with me. One of these places was our summer home in Huntsville, Utah. Whenever we went there, I felt a sense of peace.

Arleta, California was our other home, and it too held a special meaning for me. I have some wonderful memories from our time there, along with some rough moments that have stayed in my mind (not all of my memories of Arleta are good ones).

Other wonderful places that have been special to me include: Lythm-St. Anne's, Blackpool, and Ipswich in England. Still other special are Branson, Missouri; and Logan, Ogden, and Provo, Utah; and Disneyland, Sweden, and Tokyo.

After a while, it didn't matter where I was; every place had a way of feeling like home. I could be at a certain venue performing on stage or outside by a tree in England—it didn't matter. I started holding certain places in my mind as special and came to consider them "Jay's Spots." From all over the world, I have little memories of corners of buildings, gardens, rooms, and trees. The important thing for me was that these special spots were all places where I felt happy or safe. I would go to these places in my mind when I was stressed and looking for a little peace. I suppose I have "trained" myself to do this from all the years we spent on the road. I feel everyone needs to have special places that mean a lot to them, so they can "visit" them when they need to, even if only in their mind.

I have traveled so much, and have seen so many hotel rooms, that I have sometimes been fooled as to whether I'm home or on the road when I wake up. My bedroom at home resembles the structure and look of a hotel room. I do this purposely so that when I'm on the road, I can try to put myself in the frame of mind that I have when I'm at home and away from the craziness of show business. This little method can also work in the reverse—when things get crazy at home, I can go to my room and pretend I'm on the road.

Another place that has become special for me is a cruise ship. Some people would call being on a cruise ship "heaven"; however, I know a few people (believe it or not) who think being on the water is like being in "hell." It's all in our perception.

When I think about it, this is the same way some people perceive life here on earth—it can be heaven or hell. My mother used to say, "It's all how you look at it." My parents taught us, "You can create heaven on earth if you want to."

Utah State University in Logan, Utah in 1979 was one of those times when life felt like heaven to me. I had the best time of my single life there, having taken some time off from show business to be a college student. I tried to go back to that place a couple of years later to recapture those feelings, those memories, and basically relive the past. But, as I should have learned from my experience in Ogden, you can't relive old memories—you can only cherish them. When we try to "go back," we can only create new memories in the same place. I have also learned that people can be happy anywhere they are, if they have a good reason or purpose for being there.

There were many scenes in my mind that were so dramatic back in the early 1970s. Those scenes are funny to me now, but back then they were quite an ordeal. I remember having so much fun at Provo High School. I would go to dances and join in as many activities as I could. I would flirt with all the girls— especially a girl named Dana Williams. I was bugged by the fact that even though she liked me, she liked another guy, as well. I was jealous for the first time in my life.

I used to think how I longed to play football on the high school team and just wanted to be a normal kid. I remember one day, Donny and I got into a problem at the high school when we were flirting with a bunch of cheerleaders. A group of about ten guys came out of nowhere and started throwing cans and rocks at us. This really disturbed me and scared the girls, but Donny went ballistic and wanted to take them all on. Even though we were both taught by Chuck Norris and were good at karate, I realized later that we could have been "toast." Once in a great while, I drive by Provo High and have a good laugh as I think back on those times.

Act 3

~1966—1969~

ON THE ROAD

Act 3, Scene 1

EXPANDING OUR HORIZONS

Occasionally we would try a gig or two on our own. Don Williams, Andy's brother, was our new manager and wanted to help us become a little more independent in the business. Our first performance on our own was in 1963 at the Fairmont Hotel in San Francisco, California. Unfortunately, only two people showed up. We were pretty upset, and our father was quite embarrassed. He tried to get us out of the date, but we had to go on because the two people who came refused to leave. We performed our show with just the waiters, the technical crew and that couple (who, by the way, loved the show). The next day was better—about eight people showed up. Our engagement at the Fairmont was a very humbling experience, and a memorable one.

Andy Williams, the Moon River Moth

As everyone knows, Andy Williams is famous for the song Moon River. We sang background with him on that song many times. I'll never forget performing with Andy at the Illinois State Fair around 1965. Just off to the side of the stage I saw a moth . . . and it was headed right in Andy's direction. Next thing I know, I hear Andy singing, "Mooooooon riiiiiverrrrr"—and the moth flew into his throat! Poor Andy coughed his way all the way through that last note. It was at that moment I realized my idol was only human! Maybe this is when my phobia of moths began.

A Flight of Terror

I'll also never forget a particular flight we took to perform in New Mexico when I was about 10 years old. To get to the show, we took two Beechcraft airplanes, which each sat about 10–12 people. My brothers, my father, and I were in one of the planes; and flying just ahead of us in the other plane were Andy and some of the band members. All of a sudden we saw a big spark and heard a terrible pop on the right side of our plane. The engine was on fire! Our pilot was amazing as he shut it down and feathered the remaining engine so that we could make an emergency landing at a nearby airport. It was a terrible landing and quite a traumatic experience for me. Andy's plane landed at that same airport, and we all got on his plane for the rest of the trip. It is amazing to me now to look back and think about going through all of that as youngsters—how we managed to put it all aside and perform a show that night like nothing traumatic had happened. That was certainly the epitome of the cliché, "The show must go on."

Sweden

The country of Sweden holds very special memories for our family. Don Williams had a connection with several venues there, especially with Lars (Lasse) Lönndahl—Sweden's most popular singer. This presented our family with the wonderful opportunity to spend the summers of 1966, 1967, 1968 and 1969 (Marie joined us that summer) performing at Liseberg Park in Gothenburg, as well as other folk parks around Sweden. We also did some television shows and even recorded a couple of albums in Swedish with one of their record labels. We met and got reacquainted with Louis Armstrong there (who also appeared on the first show we did for Disney). We worked hard, played hard, and learned a lot about balance while we were in Sweden. We had so much fun—I think all of my brothers, and my sister, would agree these were the best summers of our childhood.

Alan and Water Don't Always Mix

Don Williams booked us to perform at a fair in Washington in the late 1960s. Our act was performed in between their horse races. It had just rained and there were puddles everywhere on the stage. We were wearing tap shoes and were going to be performing a number with guitars, etc. We got onstage and Alan yelled to the crowd, "Hey! How are you doing!?" He then proceeded to step into a puddle, and the metal on the bottom of his tap shoes caused an electric current to shoot through him, which resulted in him jumping about five feet into the air like one of Jerry Lewis's comedic characters. Alan can definitely attest that water and electricity don't mix.

Our Days with the Rodeo

During that same time frame, Don booked us with a rodeo where the bull got loose. It rained at this event, too, and the stage was just a plank of wood in the middle of a lot of mud. When that bull got loose, he began to run around the stage. When the song's tempo picked up, the bull stopped and stared at us. I swear that bull was watching the show; the rodeo clowns couldn't even get it to move. It reminded me of the time we were in Sweden and a donkey from a nearby petting zoo came to the front of the stage as we performed. So, the bull in our audience brought back some other outrageous, happy, and fun memories. I guess you could say we've performed for some tough crowds.

Japan

During the spring seasons of 1967–69, we went to Japan to perform with Pat Boone and his daughters (Debby Boone and I had a mutual crush on each other back then). This was another interesting time for us. In addition to performing with the Boone family, we also did television commercials for the popular Japanese health drink called "Calpis." It was challenging to pretend to like something that actually tasted terrible (I hope that opinion isn't offensive to my Japanese friends)! We also did many interviews in Japan, and Jimmy was the star of "The Osmonds" there. He was actually the first one in our family to receive a gold record. Jimmy picked up the language naturally and was able to converse with the interviewers in Japanese.

I remember when we were guests on a comedy television special where we portrayed a group of prisoners locked in a jail cell. It was really a funny routine, except that we had to work on Christmas Day. The next day, Jimmy broke his arm in a revolving door at the Tokyo Hilton. Another time, a television host asked Merrill what instrument he played. Merrill replied, "The banjo," and the audience broke into laughter. They thought he said "benjou," which refers to the bathroom in Japanese. Our time spent in Japan is quite a memory for all of us.

Embarrassing the Queen

Merrill has had some embarrassing moments in the press. One time while in England, we were performing for the Queen. This was our first command performance for her, and we were performing with other guests, including Rowan and Martin (from the television show *Laugh-In*), Liza Minnelli, and Roger Moore (who played James Bond for many years). At the end of the show, it is customary for the Queen to shake hands with the performers. When she got to Merrill, he was so nervous that he wet his lips as the photographers were taking pictures of him with the Queen. The next day, newspaper headlines read, "Osmond sticks tongue out at the Queen."

It is almost overwhelming to think about all of the amazing opportunities we had at such a young age. I know every bit of it played a part in our growth and development as a family, and for me as an individual.

By this time, we were teenagers and felt we needed to "spread our wings" and move into the record scene. Andy Williams had a record label, Barnaby Records, and helped us get started recording. After a while, Jerry Goldstein, the producer for the group War, talked us into moving to Uni Records. Andy gave us his blessing as we embarked on a new chapter of our careers. We wanted to expand and no longer be labeled as "Andy's boys." We wanted to show the world we could do other things.

Act 3, Scene 2

HOME AWAY FROM HOME, AWAY FROM HOME

Our home in Huntsville, Utah was a place of peace. It was built by our Uncle Ralph while we were living in Ogden in 1958. It was intended to be a summer home for us. It was our second home no matter where else we were living at the time. Our home in Ogden was turned into a rental property, so when we weren't living in California, we spent our time in Huntsville.

We loved going to Huntsville. It was a getaway from everything, and those times still hold such wonderful memories for me. Every time we would get on that old dirt road to the house, we would all sing together in the car, "Almost There," the song performed by Andy Williams in the movie, *I'd Rather Be Rich*.

I've lived in a lot of different places, so I certainly won't go into all of them. I think the moves during my youth were the most pivotal for me. In the fall of 1962, we were renting a little house in Santa Ana, California for a few months. At the time, we thought we'd only be on *The Andy Williams Show* for two or three episodes. After working on those few episodes, we moved to Canoga Park, California (where Jimmy was born). An overwhelming response came in from Andy's viewers, and we were asked to continue working on the show for a longer period of time. That change in plans brought about the move for us from Canoga Park to Arleta, California at the end of 1963.

During our years with Andy Williams, I realized we were on an unusual journey as a family, and I started feeling different than other kids. However, I loved it when I went to school in Canoga Park, and I also loved Liggett Street Elementary School in Arleta, California, where I went to school in 1964 for a short time. Going to public school made me feel like a normal kid. There was a lot of traveling back and forth, so I also had tutors at the NBC studio during *The Andy Williams Show.* I didn't like being tutored, though I tried hard to do my assignments in between rehearsals. This, however, proved to be very difficult. I started longing to be "normal" and to stay in public school. I was so torn by this challenge but realized later that it turned out to be a blessing. That desire to want to be in a public school setting and to feel like a normal kid is what caused me to want to go to college later on in life. My mother always wanted us to have a good education, which is one of the reasons education has always been very important to me. With a career in entertainment not being conducive to working towards a college degree, reaching my goal of a degree would take a while— but is something I would never let up on.

LAUGHS WITH JERRY LEWIS

In 1968, we were no longer regulars on *The Andy Williams Show* but still made occasional guest appearances. We were asked to perform quite a few times on *The Jerry Lewis Show.* We ended up being almost regulars on his show for two years. We were told to be creative and bring the same kind of variety to the show that we did on *The Andy Williams Show.* Of course, we said we could do it and broadened our skills using gymnastics, comedy sketches, and more instruments.

Working with Jerry Lewis allowed me to see two sides of him —the funny man and a very serious person. (It seems to me that most comedians have a very serious side that not a lot of people get to see.) We never knew what mood Jerry would be in, but there was never a shortage of laughs when he wanted to be crazy. One time, when my brothers and I were about to record our saxophone number (which was a complicated piece and required serious effort), Jerry came into our recording session, took our sheet music, and set it on fire. We hadn't memorized that music, yet, and wondered if our number just went up in smoke. We actually had to reconstruct the whole thing. Jerry was notorious for interrupting, and I never knew how nutty a person could be until we worked with him. He could be sulking one minute and crazy the next. I learned so much while we worked with Jerry—he really stretched our imaginations. That is when I learned about what it takes to put together comedy sketches. Donny had a hilarious part where he played the son of "Ralph Rotten" (one of Jerry's characters). Another comedy sketch that really stands out in my mind is when we sang "Danny Boy." The harmony was really tight on this song—so that part was serious—but Jerry conducted the number, which made it really funny.

This was all happening at the same time Alan decided to go into the National Guard. When Alan went into the Army in 1968, it was quite an adjustment for us as a group. He felt a duty to serve the country, and we were determined to support that. Alan's absence put us through a lot of different dynamics, and I really saw how his leadership had affected us. Wayne didn't want to "officially" be the group's leader. Merrill didn't want to fill Alan's shoes, either, but eventually stepped into the role while Alan was away.

Working with Jerry Lewis was one of the most challenging yet fun times of my career. Most of all, we learned there was still a lot to the entertainment industry that we had yet to explore.

WHAT HAPPENS IN VEGAS

I've always disliked the old cliché, "What happens in Vegas stays in Vegas." I feel we are all accountable for our actions regardless of where we are, and our actions follow us.

We'd been performing in Las Vegas since 1963. Our first gig there was at the Sahara Hotel with Don Rickles. Later, we performed at the Desert Inn with Phyllis Diller, and then we did a few shows at The Frontier with Phil Harris.

In Vegas, our audiences were different from those whom we performed for at other venues. It was obviously a different atmosphere, and there were different pressures. For instance, this period of time was before smoking regulations. At every performance we could see a cloud of smoke rising above our audience and onto the stage. Unfortunately, we had to deal with the smoke two shows per night. It really was an unhealthy situation. Today, we use fog machines for effects on stage, but back then we didn't need to—that effect was already there from the ever-present smoke hanging in the air.

We continued to perform in Vegas on a fairly regular basis into the 1970s. Aside from working with Andy Williams and Jerry Lewis at Caesars Palace, we also performed with Nancy Sinatra at the International Hotel (now the Hilton). We went to Vegas three or four times a year for several weeks at a time.

I remember a time when we were doing a difficult dance routine with Nancy on stage. She tripped over my brother Alan, and really took a bad fall. She was highly embarrassed (especially with her father in the audience, which is probably why she was so mad). She blamed Alan and really told him off when we were backstage. Frank came backstage and immediately diffused the situation by assuring all of us that everything was okay. He seemed like a really cool guy.

It was when we worked in Vegas that we became acquainted with Frank Sinatra; he had a genuine respect for our family—especially our parents.

A lot of people don't know this, but Frank Sinatra was the first one to donate to the Osmond Foundation. He believed in my parents' cause and once told them that if they held true to their dream of helping kids, big things could happen—and he was right!

Another time when we worked with Nancy in Vegas, there was a part in our show where Jimmy did an imitation of Frank. He was just a little guy at the time, about seven or eight years old, and he wore a hat that Frank had previously given him. Jimmy sang "That's Life," imitating the legend. I'll never forget the look on Frank Sinatra's face as he watched Jimmy impersonating him. Frank gave Jimmy a big standing ovation that night.

Jimmy also sang Elvis's songs, "Trouble" and "I Got a Woman," in our show, and my brothers and I backed him up instrumentally. One night, just before the start of our show, we were told Elvis was in the light booth watching us. Can you imagine the pressure? Jimmy went on stage like a trooper and sang his heart out. We could see Elvis enjoying the show—especially Jimmy's performance. However, Jimmy was so nervous that he threw up into the lap of a lady sitting in the front row. What a night!

We became good friends with Elvis shortly after we started headlining at Caesars Palace. On our days off, we would go to The International Hotel and catch his shows. He would insist we go backstage and hang out with him. To me, he seemed somewhat lonely. I think, in a way, Elvis needed a sense of family, and that is probably what he saw in us. He really admired our parents. Everyone knew how much Elvis missed his own mother, and what better mother to fill that void a little than Olive Osmond?

Elvis would invite us to parties at his penthouse at the International Hotel—his home away from home. Elvis was quite a pinball freak, and had seven or eight pinball machines in his penthouse (that is when I got hooked on pinball). When we were in town, we would often go to see Elvis perform, and he'd invite us to his dressing room for a visit. It was during one of those visits that he talked us into using his designer, Bill Belew, to create those unforgettable white, dazzling jumpsuits we wore in the 1970s. I will never forget a particular occasion when one of Elvis's band members hit a bad note during the show. Elvis stopped the song and jokingly said, "If you can't do it right, I'm going to invite the Osmonds to take your place!" Of course, I felt bad for the band member but also thought how cool it was that we were just paid such a huge compliment by Elvis Presley.

Elvis's backup vocalists, The Jordanaires, along with his band also accompanied us a few times when we worked with Nancy Sinatra at The International. That is when I got to know his drummer, Ronnie Tutt, who later traveled with us on the road and became quite an influence on my drumming.

Elvis told us to always be sure to show our appreciation for our fans, because they helped put us where we were in our careers. We never forgot his advice and will never forget him.

During these years, as we learned about the respect these great performers had for us, it helped give us a little boost of confidence. So many skeptics at the time said we weren't cool enough for this business because of our "squeaky clean" image; but if Elvis Presley and Frank Sinatra thought we were cool, we felt we were doing something right and it didn't matter what the skeptics thought.

I think those experiences in Vegas enriched our careers, earned us some respect in the field of entertainment, and prepared us for how to handle all that comes with being in the business. What happened in Vegas didn't stay there—we took it with us.

Act 4

~1970—1975~

LIFE BECOMES A WHIRLWIND

ANOTHER FACET

In 1970 we were offered the opportunity to be part of *Disneyland Showtime's Haunted Mansion.* It was fun working with Kurt Russell again; he was like one of my brothers. It was great to work with E. J. Peaker on the project, as well. It took a good month to shoot this show; and at one point, they even closed Disneyland for a day so we could film without disruption. Think about the fun a bunch of kids could have in Disneyland with no one else around. What a day! We played football on Main Street in between scenes, went on rides by ourselves during our lunch breaks, and went through the Haunted Mansion backwards. Kurt accidentally fell down an open pit and really got hurt—it was amazing he didn't break anything. The director was worried our craziness could result in more injuries and insisted future adventures through the Haunted Mansion take place with the lights on. The ride wasn't the same after that.

It was a great experience to try our hand at acting again, but I found that I felt more comfortable singing on stage with my brothers. Part of the movie entailed performing on Disneyland's Tomorrowland stage (which has since been torn down) with Kurt Russell as emcee.

While we were there, Olivia Newton-John visited with us. Alan had a major crush on her, and I think she may have liked him, as well. I tagged along with Alan and Olivia around Disneyland, and I'll never forget our ride on the Pirates of the Caribbean. Olivia sat in between Alan and me. When we hit the ride's first dip, Olivia turned towards my right ear and screamed a scream like I've never heard before. I know I lost decibels in that ear! That, however, wasn't the worst of it. Olivia proceeded to dig her fingernails into my skin and actually drew blood. This all happened within two seconds time. I love her, but whenever I hear her name, I think of my own little nickname for her—"Olivia Nightmare-John."

William Shatner and his family also came to see us perform at Disneyland in 1969 while we were filming *The Haunted Mansion*. This was when *Star Trek* was at its peak, and I was quite a "Trekky." Being such a *Star Trek* fan, I again experienced one of those weird moments where I had to separate the world of television from reality. Disneyland is the perfect place to mix the two together.

The daughters of Pat Boone and Rory Calhoun (the famous cowboy actor) also visited us while we were filming. After we finished shooting for the day, they'd go on rides with us and we'd all have a great time together.

It seemed like those days of filming *The Haunted Mansion* went by really fast. It was an honor to be a part of the opening of *The Haunted Mansion*; but more than that, it was just fun to be at the place where it all happened for us a few years prior.

Whenever I go to Disneyland, I love to go into City Hall and reminisce about our audition for Walt Disney. He had a little apartment right above the fire station. I like to walk down Main Street and visualize the crowds gathering to listen to our little barbershop quartet and remember how we would get complimentary Sunkist orange juice for singing. Most of all, I love to visit the statue of Walt Disney and Mickey Mouse that stands in front of the famous "Sleeping Beauty Castle" and remember the autographed drawing Walt Disney did just for me. Disneyland will always remain truly a magical place in my mind.

Singing & Dancing

"Prepare yourself and the opportunity will come." My mother loved this phrase, and I remember her using it often. Those words paid off for us many times. One of the people who helped to get us prepared for meeting Walt Disney was Val Hicks. He was our fist vocal coach. Val listened to us sing at our first paid performance at the convention for Wheeler Machinery in Salt Lake City. Afterwards, he told our father that we had a natural blend; and he believed that with some vocal coaching, we could really fine-tune our talents. Father hired him to teach us some songs, and that relationship led to our becoming connected to the Barbershop Harmony Society, which, in turn, led us to their convention in Kansas City in 1960. We were projected to be their future champs in barbershop. Val groomed us so we'd be ready when we finally got our big break into the business with Walt Disney. In the 1960s, George Wyle took us to the next level on *The Andy Williams Show*. With his understanding of harmonies and vocal parts, my brothers and I developed a special way of singing that quickly became as natural for us as speaking. (By the way, George wrote the tune for the *Gilligan's Island* television show.) He took us from barbershop harmony into harmonies singing with a band. Earl Brown took over after George. He also had a big influence on us as a group, as he worked to deepen our blend and make our harmonies become more intricate. We learned to listen, improvise, juggle parts, and buzz chords (harmonies so tight, you could almost hear a buzz between them). Our first Christmas album was all Earl Brown's influence.

Of course, along with singing on *The Andy Williams Show* was dancing. Virl and Tom helped us learn our tap dancing routines since they were taking lessons around the same time we were trying to learn tap dancing for *The Andy Williams Show*. When we would go home from California, we would be taking both singing lessons from Val Hicks and dance lessons from Virl, Tom, and the Dias family. Shortly thereafter, we began to work with Nick Castle, our first choreographer (he worked with Fred Astaire, Gene Kelly, and Shirley Temple—and has 85 films to his credit). Jack Regas later took over as our choreographer. He taught us the dance routine referred to as "Fascinating Rhythm," which we used until around 1995. He and his family became great friends of ours (Jack later became one of the all-time great directors). Then, Jimmie Rogers (who danced in the movie, *West Side Story*), taught us routines that were even more difficult. He included karate moves and gymnastics. This is evident to those who remember the difficult dance routine we did on *The Flip Wilson Show* when we performed the song, "Yo-Yo."

The knowledge we received from these great vocal coaches and choreographers enhanced our skills greatly. Even though they were all tough at times, I'll never forget the great expertise and training we received from each of them.

BEHIND THE HITS

Toward the end of 1969, we recorded a number of songs with Uni Records. Bill Cowsill and other record producers were trying to get us a hit. We were starting to see some chart action, but nothing big. Our contract with Uni was up at the end of that year, and right after the contract was finished we got a call from our friend Mike Curb. Mike was President of MGM Records then, and he said he had a great idea for us. He wanted us to fly to Alabama to meet Rick Hall, an R&B record producer who was confident he could help us get a hit record.

Father, Alan, Wayne, Merrill, Donny and I flew to Muscle Shoals, Alabama. It was a beautiful area and very laid back. This was a brand new world for me. Mike Curb and Rick Hall strongly believed in the Osmond Brothers, despite what key record people were saying about us at the time.

I'll never forget the first time we listened to the demo song, "One Bad Apple." We were in Rick's office at the FAME Recording Studios, and at the very same moment, each of us felt it was a hit song.

I'll also never forget the day our family was gathered around the radio listening to Casey Kasem (the famous radio personality), as he hosted his weekly national top countdown radio show. Casey said, "Now, here's the number one song in America—'One Bad Apple' by The Osmonds!" Wayne, in his excitement, took off running; Marie screamed; my brothers started yelling and play fighting; Father and Mother hugged each other; and I just sat there on the couch . . . amazed at what had just happened to this little Mormon family from Ogden, Utah.

Once "One Bad Apple" hit number one, we began receiving a lot of offers. Ray Katz, Ed Lefler and Jim Morey were our managers at the time. Dick Clark (host of *American Bandstand*) and his concert promotions company were our new agents and began setting up our concert tours. Peggy Rogers was the agent in charge. She was amazing at her job and handled all of the details for those crazy tours. Our first big concert was in Cleveland, Ohio. Before the concert, we were the Grand Marshalls in their parade. I couldn't believe all that was happening in our lives. The concert that night will forever be in my mind. It was sold out, and the reaction of the screaming girls was unbelievable. It was like a roar of thunder with flashes everywhere as the concert hall went dark. We were led on stage by a flashlight, and Alan was at the back of the line so he couldn't see the edge of stage. As we turned, he went straight forward and fell off the stage. My brothers and I got set, plugged in, and waited for Alan's cue to start the music. There was no cue, there was no Alan, and we had no idea what had happened to him. Finally he hobbled onto stage, gave the cue, and the show began. The whole evening was very intense and amazing. I'll never forget it.

This is just a sampling of a typical tour for us in the 1970s (details expertly arranged by Peggy Rogers):

1972 World Tour

July 21	Akron Rubber Bowl	Akron, OH
Aug. 4	Schaefer Stadium	Foxboro, MA
Aug. 5	Memorial Auditorium	Syracuse, NY

Aug. 6–7	Allentown Fairgrounds	Allentown, PA
Aug. 8	Baltimore Civic Auditorium	Baltimore, MD
Aug. 10	Nashville Auditorium	Nashville, TN
Aug. 11	Garrett College	Montgomery, AL
Aug. 12	Rickwood Field	Birmingham, AL
Aug. 13	City Park Stadium	New Orleans, LA
Aug. 15	Torrant Coliseum	Ft. Worth, TX
Aug. 17	Kansas City Auditorium	Kansas City, MO
Aug. 18	State Fairgrounds	Des Moines, IA
Aug. 19	Sports Arena	Minneapolis, MN
Aug. 21	Milwaukee Coliseum	Milwaukee, WI
Aug. 24–26	Garden State Arts Festival	Holmdel, NJ
Aug. 28–29	Ohio State Fair	Columbus, OH
Sept. 8	Angel Stadium	Anaheim, CA

My Time to Shine

We were in Los Angeles, California, and I received a call from *Soul Train,* which was a big television dance show back in the 1970s. It was similar to Dick Clark's *American Bandstand,* only it appealed more to a black audience. I felt honored that the producer said Chaka Khan's sister, Yvonne Stevens ("Taka Boom") saw me dancing with my brothers and wanted to invite me to dance with her on the show. I wore my favorite Hawaiian shirt and danced my legs off. Even though I stuck out like a sore thumb, I had a great time. It was from this show that I realized how fun dancing could be. I wanted to take the moves I learned that night, continue learning, and incorporate soul moves into our songs and routines. I eventually took my love for dancing and became the Osmond Brothers' official choreographer. I took this to another level and became Donny and Marie's choreographer, as well. Through my exposure to dance over the years, I developed a real interest to once again stretch. I produced and staged the opening numbers and concert spots for *The Donny & Marie Show.* The concert spots were called, "Little Bit Country/Little Bit Rock 'n' Roll." Not only was I in charge of the choreography for those segments, but I was also responsible for the music Donny and Marie sang and Donny's stage effects. After all these years, it is fun to still be called on to add a few moves to our act from time to time.

AGAINST ALL ODDS

The odds for our family to get a hit record in the 1970s were slim. The drug culture really infiltrated the music world at that time. It was not a family-oriented business, and some of the top record executives in the industry were telling us we weren't going to make it unless we "got hip." We knew we had our work cut out for us and that the squeaky clean image was going to be a challenge, but we persevered and eventually prevailed.

It was again a big shock when our next two songs, "Double Lovin'" and "Yo-Yo" hit the charts—both in the top five. It felt surreal to each of us, and eventually the pressure to maintain was on. We were very much into recording and trying to find that next hit song. That's when my brothers started to write music. I actually was involved in most of their writing sessions. I was always providing the rhythm on the drums, which led to the chorus, then the verse, the lyrics—and the song.

The pressures of the spotlight started to outweigh the success. This was another time in my life when I wanted to feel "normal" like any other teenager. On one hand I was grateful for the success we had, but on the other, it was a burden that carried some daunting internal feelings and responsibilities. There was also an uneasiness I felt with adulation (it still makes me uncomfortable to this day). I didn't want to feel different, but I knew we were and felt very torn as a result. I liked the limelight some of the time but really enjoyed the peace and comfort of normality.

I learned early on that a career in show business is very much like riding a rollercoaster—there are ups, and there are downs. I knew for us to sustain in this business we needed to learn to ride the rollercoaster with dignity.

Back in the 1970s, the people who really ran the show for us were Bill Sammeth, Ron Clark, Dick Callister, and Jim Morey. Billy "Fish" Sammeth was one of the key players that led to the success of our family. He made the first contacts to a great person by the name of Nola Leoni (*16 Magazine* Editor), and then to others in the teen magazine world. This brought fans in touch with us, which was a wonderful vehicle to provide access and information about our family.

Ron Clark took over media affairs and protected the family's image throughout the 1970s and 80s. We owe much of our success to Ron and felt we could literally put our lives in his hands. His wife, Kathy, became close to our family, as well. To this day, Ron directs any major family event we do and represents our entire family when stressful situations are upon us.

Dick Callister was the man in charge of setting up all of the feeder companies to our television studio, as well as our other business dealings in the 1970s. His organization was designed to keep the studio afloat and our investments growing. Even though we had some tough dealings with him, I will always be grateful for the lessons I learned as a result.

Jim Morey was one of three personal managers for the family throughout the 1970s. Ray Katz and Ed Lefler were nice (our other two personal managers), but our family really took to Jim. He was "Mr. Class." We had tremendous trust in his abilities and opinions. Jim always seemed to do the right thing. His wife, Trudi, was also wonderful, and we felt like the two of them were a part of our family.

Don't Mess with Chuck Norris

In the early 1970s, we were all into karate. Elvis told us that karate contributed to his unique style. We had followed his advice on the jumpsuits and decided to incorporate karate into our act, as well. We were introduced to Chuck Norris, who had a number of karate schools (before he became really famous). We asked him if he would teach us karate, and he was very helpful. We became green belts under his system of teaching and asked him to help us choreograph a karate/fight number to drum beats that we could put into our act. As some may remember, this number resulted in the breaking of my nose on stage in front of around 18,000 people at the Indiana State Fair in 1973. I didn't get a kick out of that incident, to say the least!

I remember Chuck telling us about his movie ideas and his desire to become an actor. He was determined to pursue his dreams, and his story is truly amazing. He really is everything people say he is. He has a heart of gold but is tough as nails. One time I caught him off-guard, and the lesson I learned will always be an interesting memory for me. He was explaining to us that you need to use your peripheral vision to the point where you almost have eyes in the back of your head. He taught us about the importance of "feeling" someone behind you in case of an attack. So, I wanted to see if he could sense me "attacking" him from behind when he wasn't expecting it. He was talking to one of my brothers and I did a flying round-kick to his back. He caught me in mid-air (right after I kicked him) and turned my ankle—flipping me in the air. He then gave me a "Scotch blessing" I will never forget. From this incident I learned (and did I learn!) it isn't wise to take Chuck Norris by surprise.

Jim Morey, Starring in "Psycho"

I called Jim "Morey Man." He was quite a character and really made it fun to be on the road. Jim's quick wit and steady manner gave me a much-needed stability to handle problems as they came along. My parents always taught me to roll with the punches, and Jim was a great example of just how to do that. Jim had a weakness, though, and made the mistake of revealing what it was to Donny and me. He admitted that the Alfred Hitchcock movie, *Psycho,* terrified him. Donny and I put our heads together and concocted a great scheme. One day we phoned the hotel we were headed to and asked the manager to find a mannequin with arms extended. We went into detail how we wanted the manager to tape a knife in the mannequin's hands, put a wig on it, and stand it in the shower of Jim's room with the water turned on. We also asked for a bucket of water to be placed in the room. The hotel manager did what we asked and had everything ready for Jim when he entered his room. When we arrived at the hotel, Donny and I just had to follow Jim. We saw Jim's face turn white as a sheet when he heard the shower running. We slowly followed Jim to the bathroom with trepid anticipation. He carefully opened the shower curtain, and the scream we heard that day was probably the worst one we'll ever hear in our lives. Jim turned to run, and as a grand finale to our joke I threw the bucket of water on him. I honestly have never seen anyone run so fast or scream so loud in my life (well, then again, there was that scream from Olivia).

Panic in Memphis

We've been through a lot of unforgettable experiences over the years, including two hotel fires. One of those fires was in July 1972 at the Holiday Inn Rivermont in Memphis, Tennessee. We had just finished writing the music for *The Plan,* which would later become what we considered our concept album, and that was among the things we lost in the fire. We were in the hotel; I was with Wayne in our room. We heard someone running down the hall yelling, "Fire!" We ran out into the hall to discover complete panic. This was such a terrifying experience; I can still remember the smoke, the screaming, and not being able to see anything but the lighted exit signs above the stairwell doors. Because of the smoke and being unable to see, I lost my way as I tried to find an exit. We all kept yelling to stay down near the ground as we tried to guide each other to safety. I was so worried about where everyone was and stayed back with our parents to make sure we heard Donny, Marie, and Jimmy's voices before we headed down. I knew my older brothers could get themselves out, but I kept yelling to Donny, Marie, and Jimmy to head to the exit signs and to stay down. We got to a stairwell door, and one of our band members (John Rosenburg), who happened to be a karate expert, kicked the door open. I was so grateful when we all made it out unharmed.

Cartoons

A time that really stands out for me was 1973. This is when we had several hits in one year, tying the Beatles and Elvis on the charts. This particular year was literally a string of major events. It felt like it never stopped for one moment. The family seemed to be united and focused. We were all pulling together, despite problems of the world pulling us apart. With a lot of success comes a lot of problems. We had to learn to make the decisions that were best for the family and not for any one individual. Our attitude was "all for one and one for all." Even the decision to have Donny start a solo recording career was a family decision. This was because we all believed that it didn't matter who was out in front, as long as it was an Osmond.

In 1972, The Osmonds cartoon series, produced by Rankin-Bass Studios, aired on ABC Television. The cartoon series was really fun for us to do. Oftentimes soundalike actors would be used for programs like this, but our actual singing and speaking voices were used for our cartoon series. One particular episode stands out to me as a good depiction of what our lives actually were like at that time. The episode was the "Chinese Restaurant Taxi Getaway" and was based on a real experience at Shepherds Bush in England. Hundreds of girls were waiting for us at the television studio/theater lobby, and we had to come up with a plan to somehow make an exit. Donny played decoy, as he went to the third level of the building to wave at the girls from a window, and the girls left the lobby area to get a view of him. The rest of us then went to the lobby where the girls had been and ducked down on our hands and knees. There was a brick wall about four or five feet high that we crawled along, with about 500 screaming girls just on the other side of it. We had a plan that had two taxies waiting outside a nearby Chinese restaurant. The brick wall led to the restaurant, so we crawled our way to the restaurant, then ran through it and out to the taxies. We figured we'd then be decoys for Donny, so when the girls saw us, they'd leave their vantage point thinking he was coming down to get in the taxies with us. Donny made a mad dash from the third floor to the lobby, where his taxi was waiting just outside. The rest of us jumped into the two taxies waiting outside the Chinese restaurant, but we soon discovered a little glitch in our plan. The one taxi driver was a part of the plan and knew what to do, but the other taxi we got into wasn't a part of the plan. It turned out that Merrill and I got into the wrong taxi. Alan, Wayne, and Jimmy's driver, knowing what was going on, took off along with the taxi Donny got into. The driver of the taxi Merrill and I got into, having no idea what was going on, sat there too long—and the girls started jumping on the taxi and banging on it. Our driver thought we were caught up in some sort of violent protest and started screaming like he was going to die. Merrill and I laughed hysterically at the driver's panic attack. We asked him to lock the doors and drive slowly, and he finally got us out of there. He didn't appreciate the attack on his taxi, but we did finally get him to laugh about it. It was such a funny experience that we tried to recreate it through this cartoon episode. I watched the cartoon one time with my boys and their friends, and they couldn't believe all of that really happened to us.

There were so many unusual and actually very scary experiences that came from those days of "mania." I remember one particular time when Donny and I were in a crowd of screaming girls. We both ended up on the ground with the girls pulling at our hair and clothes. Our bodyguard was trying to pull a couple of girls off of us. I managed to get up and was looking for Donny.

I spotted him and said, "There you are!" Suddenly someone's flash cube snapped right in my eye. For three days I was blinded by that flash cube! Another time, Donny had a pen poked in his face right underneath his eye. He was lucky; the result of that could have been horrible.

Paper Airplanes and Pizzas

Donny and I tried to make being on the road as fun as possible. We would play football and run from the fans as they would chase us down the street. One time we signed pieces of paper and folded them into paper airplanes and then sailed them out the window from our hotel room balcony. The ultimate "fan tease" was the day Donny and I ordered about 15–20 uncut pizzas and thought it would be really fun to hurl them as Frisbees from our window. The hotel manager didn't find it as amusing as Donny and I did, but the fans loved having dinner on us! This fun with the fans somewhat made up for the bad feelings we had when security would overdo their jobs.

Osmondmania

One of the things my family really disagreed with was the way the security at a particular hotel in England would use water hoses on the girls for crowd control. Their security felt this practice was necessary because the screaming was overwhelming and fans would follow us into the hotel garage. So the police (Bobbies) would turn water hoses on them. They said it was the only way they knew to get the fans to back away. This was very upsetting to us. There was often frenzy in the crowds, so we knew there was a need for safety, but we never wanted our fans to feel mistreated. I guess that is why, whenever we could, Donny and I would do things to try to make up for the tight security that went along with this stage of our lives.

We finally told the hotel we'd take care of our own security. We hired what we nicknamed "Rent-a-Thugs," but it was impossible for them to keep the crowds away. So, we would get mobbed. On one particular occasion, I got out of the car, turned around, and a girl got me wedged in between the car door. In her excitement, she had me around the neck and was cutting off my airway. Girls started getting into the car and the situation became very chaotic. I couldn't breathe, and the more I tried to get away, the more the girl would squeeze. There were girls all around me; I was pinned in and couldn't move. I didn't see it, but my mother later told me she saw the girl who had a "death grip" on me and came to my rescue. My little mother lifted the girl up, which forced her to let go of my neck. One of our "Rent-a-Thugs" saw the whole thing and said he couldn't believe the strength that came out of my little mother at that moment.

So, the craziness that had become our lives took on a name: "Osmondmania." To further describe this mania, following is an excerpt from a newspaper article that looked back on a memorable day in 1972:

> "Osmondmania," by Mark J. Price
>
> *The Beacon Journal,* July 21, 2003
>
> Unless you were there, you can't begin to imagine the chaos. A high-pitched, ear-splitting wail rose above the Akron Rubber Bowl as thousands of teary-eyed girls screamed at the top of their lungs. Eeeeeeeeee!
>
> The teeny boppers trembled and cried, surging toward the stage, pledging undying love to five young men in white jumpsuits. And then, one by one, the girls began to pass out.
>
> About 20,000 fans (and a handful of skeptical parents) attended the Osmonds' concert July 21, 1972. The Osmond Brothers—Alan, Wayne, Merrill, Jay and Donny—had topped the U.S. charts and captured the hearts of America's daughters. Donny, then 14, was especially popular.
>
> The Belkin Productions show didn't start until 8:30 P.M., but the day began early for many. Linda

Brinkerhoff, 44, of Stow remembers going to the concert with her best friend. "We got ourselves all dolled up and went there at the crack of dawn," she said. "Our parents dropped us off there, and we're thinking, 'Aren't we brilliant?'" The two infatuated girls had everything planned. "We're thinking we're going to meet them and have lunch and probably come home with an engagement ring," she said. But when the girls arrived, they weren't alone. Other fans had already beat them there.

Kathy Lowery, 42, of Akron was among the early birds. She had staked out a gate with her sisters and cousin, enduring a 12-hour wait and 90-degree heat. "We were out there all day," she said. "We fried out there in the sun. It was such a hot day."

Fans killed time by telling stories, playing games, and dreaming about boys from Utah. Excitement rippled through the crowd when the teen idols arrived by bus and pulled inside a gate. Most fans didn't see a second bus arrive or notice a pretty, dark-haired girl step off. Marie Osmond, 12, still a year away from fame, was traveling with her parents, George and Olive Osmond. Brinkerhoff and a few others got to chat with her. "She was sewing and ironing on that other bus with her mother," Brinkerhoff said. "She was very nice, slightly shy at first, a little reserved. And then I think she kind of enjoyed getting a little bit of attention."

When the bowl opened at 7:00, there was a mad rush to get inside. Lowery, who had waited since morning, was dismayed. "We were at the wrong gate," she said. "We had to go behind everybody else."

Other headlines read "Osmond Terror" (Front page of *The Sun,* October 22, 1973, talking about the balcony collapse at London's Heathrow Airport when too many fans gathered to see us arrive); and "Osmonds: What a Scream!" (*Melody Maker,* November 3, 1973). And so it went with every city we performed in. Life was crazy, surreal, and we knew we were very blessed.

During the 1970s we tried a lot of crazy things to make our concerts exciting. For instance, at a concert in Earl's Court, we rigged Donny up to a cable so he could "fly" over the audience. We were the first group to use flash pots for an indoor fireworks effect. We were never afraid to try different things to make our shows fun for our audiences. I performed the song, "Some Kind of Wonderful," as a hydraulic riser lifted me and my drum set 20 feet into the air. The riser would shake, and it was exciting and horrifying at the same time. The audience seemed to like the effect, but to this day I have a fear of heights because of it. I do love the song, though.

Riviera Days

During this stage, we made the decision to move from California to Utah. We moved to a student housing complex near BYU called The Riviera Apartments, which our parents bought. Attached to the housing complex was a big office building, and we turned that office building into our home. There were interesting tunnels and a basement we converted into a recording studio— which we built ourselves. My room/office was on the main floor, which is also where my older brothers lived. Father and Mother, along with Donny, Marie, and Jimmy, lived upstairs. Virl and Tom were both married and living in Salt Lake City. Most of my social life from 1971 through 1978 was right there at The Riviera, even though we all moved to different places in the Provo area around 1977 when our studio was built. My social life still revolved around The Riviera Apartments: we organized outdoor screenings of films, had dances every other weekend, and made it absolutely fun to be at The Riviera. I would go on routine maintenance checks with the maintenance man (girls' apartments only, of course!) to meet new girls. I had the time of my life. I threw girls into the pool so frequently, they finally put up a sign that read, "Be prepared to be thrown in by Jay if you go to the pool!" The Riviera was a big social network of friends and dating. Jimmy bought the old Roy Rogers restaurant next to the apartments and turned it into his own restaurant called "Jimmy's." We've since sold The Riviera, but Jimmy still owns his property there (I believe it is now a Pizza Hut). The Riviera—good times!

Act 4, Scene 4

MY ANCHORS

In our church, every member is a missionary. However, in 1972 our family was unofficially, but officially, called by The Quorum of the Twelve Apostles to be ambassadors (or missionaries with an assignment) for The Church of Jesus Christ of Latter-day Saints. I believe this particular call from the elders of our church is what gave us direction as a family in the entertainment business. The church has blessed my life, and the lives of my family, beyond description. Programs such as Family Home Evening, Family Scripture Study, Family Prayer, and Home Teaching are strongly endorsed by the church. The church has given our family stability and strength to cope with the many challenges of life and has been an anchor for us. President Lee (then the first counselor in the First Presidency of the church in 1972) told our family that we needed to be aware that we were representatives of the church and for the Lord. The world was watching us, and many people might judge the church by our example. He gave us wonderful counsel and encouragement. He also warned us to avoid situations that could result in making bad choices. He told us there will always be two choices in life—one will bring us closer to God, the other will take us away from Him. His advice was to always choose that which will bring us closer to God, whether it be the friends we keep, the places we go, or what we read and watch. He also encouraged us to stand up for what we believed in; and if we did, we would always be blessed. I felt a great sense of responsibility, and a positive lift, to be a good example for the church and for families after that meeting.

Standing for Something

One of the times our family went to Germany, we were met at the airport by a lady who represented our record company. She said it was her job to make sure we had a great time while in Germany. She took us to several different places, and we ended up at a little place known for its famous folk songs and dances. It was also known for its 101 different kinds of German beer. We were each placed at a different table, sort of far from each other; and all night long the servers and people at the various tables kept saying things like, "You've got to try this beer, and this one . . . nobody will know, there's nobody watching . . . try this . . . taste this." Father became perturbed and said, "Apple juice will be just fine, thank you." It was so funny the next day when we got on the plane and saw a newspaper heading that read, "Osmonds prefer apple juice to German beer."

Anchors

Roy Disney also said something that has always stuck with me, "It is easy to make important decisions when we know what our values are." The more good choices we make, the more opportunities we will have to make more good choices.

Being in the spotlight was, and still is, a mission for my family. The only problem with fame is the risk you take of pride entering your life and changing your perception of reality. Two other great anchors in life besides the church have been my parents. Our father made sure we focused on the work and left pride out of the mix. In fact, using the word "proud" is something our father always avoided. He even took the dictionary and blacked out the word in the book. He instead would use the word "pleased." Father also had a different meaning for the word "success." To him it was a progression towards a worthy ideal, not a means to an end. He believed that everyone is a success as long as they are moving forward with their goals.

My father was loved by everyone he met. One moment he would be conversing with the janitor at a hotel and having a few laughs; the next moment he would be meeting some top executive of a billion-dollar company. When the Prophet Spencer W. Kimball dedicated the Osmond Television Studio in 1977, he personally told me my parents were not ordinary parents and that I should be grateful to have them in my life. I have always been thankful for them. I know they are still with us and are watching over us. When my father turned 65, I asked him if he was going to retire. He said, "Are you kidding? This is now my refinement stage of life. Life is just getting exciting!" Father had a hard time when Mother was very ill. He struggled to see her in such pain. He was by her bedside most of the last two years of her life. I remember him trying to joke with her one night. Mother said to him (in her sweet little raspy voice), "George, just when you get it, you gotta go." Those two wonderful people certainly created a heaven on earth. Death, a necessary part of life, was just the next step (or stage) for them.

Act 5

~1976—1979~

BEHIND THE SCENES

THE DONNY & MARIE SHOW

A new opportunity set the stage for a big change in our careers, and that opportunity put the focus on Donny and Marie. *The Donny & Marie Show* aired weekly on ABC television from 1975–1979. I really "stretched" during *The Donny & Marie Show*. This was a time in my life, as well as for my brothers (Alan, Wayne, and Merrill), to expand our talents in show business and become producers. I was in charge of all opening numbers, including the choreography and music. I was also responsible for the segment of the show called, "Little Bit Country/Little Bit Rock 'n' Roll." The pressures were immense, and I took the job very seriously. If I took on anything else at that time, I would have popped! I not only choreographed the songs for those segments, but I also programmed the music, checked the lyrics, staged the effects for Donny, and helped Art Fisher direct the camera shots. Working as a producer and choreographer on *The Donny & Marie Show* gave me a whole different perspective of show business that I didn't have before. It also gave me a voice that I didn't previously have in the group. I was in charge, and it felt invigorating. Even though I never asked for a penny for my work, it gave me a niche and purpose that motivated me. My brother Alan was in charge of the crazy finales for the show. Wayne oversaw the audio recording, and Merrill interfaced with the managers and guest stars. My youngest brother Jimmy had a difficult task. Because he was the cute little guy, and extremely talented, he was stuck with all of the tough parts such as comedy sketches and specialty numbers with puppets. We all have a good laugh now and then when Jimmy shows the videos of these performances to his kids.

Behind the Scenes

Even though the brothers periodically appeared on *The Donny & Marie Show*, it was more fun at that time to be behind the cameras, with the exception of doing a few songs, such as "Check It Out" and "Your Smiling Face." These numbers gave me the challenge of performing on my own, but I still didn't want to pursue being on my own—without my brothers.

Over the years, I've often been asked if I felt a void when we went from performing regularly as the Osmond Brothers to working behind the scenes on *The Donny & Marie Show*. I really didn't. I was taking a break, in a sense, from the hard grind of performing and traveling. We were living in California during the first two years of the show; and even though it was hard work, it was just pure fun. I even spent some time flirting on the set with Wonder Woman (Linda Carter, who was filming on the next set). When the show moved to Utah, I stopped working as a producer for the show, and became a "girl scout." Actually, I started losing interest in producing and focused on dating girls full-time when I was home in Utah and off tour.

My brothers Alan and Merrill really enjoyed producing, while Wayne didn't like it at all. If he had his way, the group would have never released "Puppy Love" or "Go Away Little Girl," and we would have stuck it out as a rock band.

If our careers hadn't taken a turn due to *The Donny & Marie Show*, I think things would have unfolded quite differently. I do believe the family decision for Alan, Wayne, Merrill, and me to work behind the scenes on *The Donny & Marie Show* hurt our performing careers as brothers, but it was a decision we all made together. We knew the chance we were taking and the sacrifices it would require, but our growth and development as producers were immense. Musically, we were all rockers at heart. The Osmond Brothers had just released the rock song, "Hold Her Tight," on which we also played the instruments. But, our image and the decision to work on *The Donny & Marie Show* counteracted our music to the rock press, and the turn of events eventually took all of us in different directions.

Alan and Merrill were expanding their talents as they pushed into other fields of business. Wayne pursued a career in flying. Donny and Marie became "Teen Sensations," and Virl and Tom moved along with their businesses in advertising and printing. Later, Tom got a job with the U.S. Postal Service, which has been a blessing in his life. Jimmy became an entrepreneur and really grew as an individual. His "cute little boy" image didn't hurt him a bit. He may disagree, but that image launched him as a unique commodity into the Japanese and English markets and into the hearts of millions of fans around the world.

On a personal level, I was in a quandary. I was not interested in the business aspect of the entertainment industry, because that all seemed way out of my control. I was in my twenties and somewhat of a "late bloomer." I think my parents were trying to get me married off, but they didn't push too hard. Jimmy, Marie, and I were the only ones not married at the time. I found myself often wandering around BYU's campus to meet girls while I audited classes—and basically was just wasting time and money. I was biding my time because I wasn't really ready to get married, yet, though I was trying (sort of) to get there. I could have a couple of Doctorate Degrees with all of the classes I've audited over the years.

Our parents were trying to focus more on letting go and watching over the younger kids. Later, they felt a need to serve the church by going on a couple of missions to England and Hawaii. They felt it was time to start helping other children to find happiness and success. They became "parents" to many.

Miss Universe Mishap

Donny was asked to guest star on the Miss Universe pageant in 1979. The pageant was held in Perth, Australia that year, and since I was working as the choreographer on *The Donny & Marie Show,* Donny insisted I go with him to help with his moves. I agreed to help him out but had an ulterior motive to meet the girls. I had a blast until Miss England told me one day that she wanted a break from the rigid schedule the contestants had. She said she cleared it with pageant officials for me to take her to lunch and that the chaperone or a pageant official was not needed. In the back of my mind I thought I should double-check that but instead agreed to pick her up. We went to lunch and then spent some time taking in the sites around Perth. I had no idea that the pageant officials were panicked that I had apparently "kidnapped" Miss England. Pageant security put out an alert with the Perth Police. We were strolling along the park in Perth, and two detectives came up and grabbed the both of us. I immediately became protective of her, because I didn't know who these guys were until they put us into a police car. They put us in their cars, and I was told, "You're in a lot of trouble, buddy!" When they called in that Miss England had been found, and who she was with, the response was, "She's with Jay Osmond!?" They were upset but not surprised. Suffice it to say I received a "Scotch blessing" for taking a contestant out without permission and without a chaperone. Pageant officials really tried to keep the story from leaking to the press, but rumors were flying around about the whole mess. Donny couldn't believe I fell for her story. I guess I couldn't believe I fell for it, either, but it is now a fun memory.

THE GRASS IS GREENER

When I was in my early twenties, I began to wonder if "the grass was greener on the other side." I already went through that silly "deprived" syndrome in my teens, thinking I missed out on a normal adolescent life. I felt for a long while that I had missed out on the teen experiences that normal adolescents have. Because my life was so different and unique, I was curious about how other people lived. This motivated me to seek out situations I perceived as normal to everyone. I called anything I considered to be a problem or challenge "a lemon." I was determined to turn these lemons (in my mind) into lemonade. I later realized these feelings became opportunities to break out of my group identity and gain a sense of independence and growth.

I created a list of everything I felt I missed out on and wanted to do. It became my "bucket list," so to speak. This included exploring whether I wanted to be in the military, play football, be a studio drummer for other bands, or work in a whole different industry. This time was when I really learned who "Jay" was. I believe so strongly that our thoughts direct our behaviors. It was because of these thoughts that I later made an attempt to pursue all of these things.

Moving to Utah

In 1976, most of my brothers were married and wanted to raise their families in Utah. *The Donny & Marie Show* was in its second season. Alan and Mother both thought it would be possible to move the show from California to Utah if we built a studio there. We took a family vote, and Wayne and I voted to stay in California—but everyone else wanted to make the move to Utah. The vote resulted in a complete lifestyle change.

As things were changing, so were we. Even though we were already invested in many real estate projects (including almond orchards in California), we chose to further expand our financial interests. We not only built our television studio in Orem, Utah, but also developed a racquetball facility with condominiums in Provo, Utah. Our recording studio at The Riviera Apartments was so well built and installed with the latest high-tech equipment, that our album, *Steppin' Out* (produced by our friend Maurice Gibb of the Bee Gee's), was recorded right there in our own studio.

Being involved in these building projects made me think I might have a talent in construction. I called our friend from Sumner Construction, and I was given a job as a construction helper for a few months. I thought I was pretty cool until I painted my room with street pavement paint. My father, who was an excellent carpenter, was somewhat upset, and so was I. I realized I had better stick with what I knew best. Even though we all tried our hand at separate things, we knew we were strong together, whatever it was. We really did show we were all for one and one for all. We knew there were several good reasons for making the move from California to Utah, and they all pointed to developing our talents and preserving our family and future together.

GI Jay

In 1978, I found myself thinking outside of the entertainment world more and more, and I wanted to try one of the things on my bucket list. I thought about how our father was such a hero in the military and decided I wanted to see if the military was something

I'd like to get into. I called Ed McMahon, who was a friend of the Osmond family. With his connections, Ed got permission from the Commandant in Washington, D.C. for me to go to Camp Williams in Utah for military training. I got be a Marine for a week. During war game activity, I was "shot" four times (which was indicated with the dropping of flags) and almost "killed" eight guys with bad aiming of my grenade launcher. (I thought I heard every curse word in the book until this.) They were very happy when I left training camp.

Houston Shoot-Out

During *The Donny & Marie Show* era, we continued to perform occasional road dates. I have quite a memory embedded in my mind from this particular time while in Houston, Texas. My brothers, sister, and I were performing at the Houston Astrodome for the Livestock & Rodeo Show. We were also filming an Osmond Family Special there at the same time. We were practicing on horses, and Donny came out "shooting pistols." There was also a spot where we practiced twirling guns and putting them into our holsters. Donny was having trouble twirling his gun and wanted to take his holster and gun back to the hotel to practice. Donny's room was two doors down the hall from mine. In between us there were a couple of people who were seriously fighting—you could hear loud banging and screaming. It was so bad that I called the hotel desk and reported the situation. All of a sudden, a gun shot went off, followed by dead quiet in the room next to me. I called the hotel desk again (as did other people), fearing that someone had been shot in the next room. The police arrived, secured the floor with guns drawn, and warned hotel guests to stay in their rooms. They banged on the door next to mine and handcuffed the couple in that room. The police conducted a search of the room, but didn't find a gun. After hours of interrogation, it was revealed that Donny accidentally shot his gun (the bullets were blanks), and an apology was made to the couple—oh, and they were also given complimentary tickets to our show.

IDENTITY STRUGGLE

The *Donny & Marie Show* later evolved into *The Osmond Family Specials.* I was starting to feel comfortable as a producer and felt more confident in making production decisions. However, when it came to the business side of things, we always made those decisions as a family. We really were a family business in every aspect. I have always viewed our family like a large company, such as General Motors. The brand "Osmond" is synonymous with family entertainment containing different sub-brands. Just as General Motors has Pontiac, Cadillac, Camero, Hummer, GM trucks, etc., we have Donny, Marie, Jimmy, Merrill, and the Osmond Brothers. Virl and Tom also played a big part in the family business in the areas of advertising, printing, and photography.

Some used to think we needed to worry about the Osmond Brothers losing their fan following while we worked behind the scenes on *The Donny & Marie Show.* I think we had a different perception of our fans than other entertainers. We thought of an "Osmond fan" as more of a "family fan"; and what one Osmond did affected all of us. I think that's one of the reasons we all stayed involved.

The Love of the Game

I was sitting in my dressing room and had just come from watching a baseball game. I looked at my brothers, who were all tired, as I was. We were getting ready to put on our costumes, and I realized there is little difference between an athlete and a performer. Whether you are tired or sick or not, you still need to go out and "play" your best. There is no room for complaining, no backing out at the last minute, and people expect a consistent performance. As I watched my brothers that night (we were all feeling a little under the weather), I developed a deeper respect for our training—because as we hit the stage it was like a light went on. That show ended up being probably one of our best performances. There was an "override button" we learned to use from our days on *The Andy Williams Show*—that the show must go on. This is professionalism, and you make it happen regardless of how you are feeling. There are some down sides, though. You learn to disengage your feelings and emotional honesty at times. In addition to being like an athlete playing his or her best, an entertainer is an actor of sorts, as well—you know the material, you know the timing, and you do the job. Sometimes in our business you have to act. A stage is an arena or forum where people want to see the "show," and this has probably been one of the hardest things I've learned as an entertainer—that sometimes you do act on stage.

Not only do actors and athletes, like performers, have to push themselves through any challenge to get the job done, but they also have to work as a team. I never had the desire to be a solo act; I've always believed we are stronger as a group. I knew that it took all of us (including the band and tech crew) to pull off a show successfully. I think back on all of the wonderful technical support team members that have blessed our lives (Ed Greene, Michael Lloyd, Allen Finlinson, Mike Williams, Mike Schaefer, Bill Waite, Chris Cole, and many, many others). Just as a baseball team needs more than just a pitcher (a first baseman is also needed, and a second and third baseman, etc.), our business of show (as my brother Jimmy refers to it) required the expertise of many to make it all happen. My thinking as I grew up was that I was one of those team players. When we were starting out, and the focus was put on me on *The Andy Williams Show,* at first I liked it; but then I felt somewhat uncomfortable, because I didn't want to be singled out. It takes all of us to make it work—that, I believe, is when we're strongest.

Quarterback Optionitist

I grew up in a very controlled environment. I struggled with making decisions on my own and then following through with them. I called it "optionitist." In my late teens, the struggle was mainly because so many people were in charge of our lives. I couldn't make personal plans, because professional decisions and work schedules always seemed to override them. I decided the only way to deal with being controlled and to not feel helpless or disappointed was to develop the skill of using options. I needed to get control of my life.

When I finally decided to break from the controlling hands of the agents and managers around me, and went to Utah State University in 1979, it was like a dream come true. Having played football as a quarterback, I related my life to a football game. A quarterback has options. If one receiver is covered, he looks to another. If that is covered, he goes to a third option. My life was the same way. I would look at one situation and if it didn't go the way I wanted, I would move on to the next option. This thought process became my way of avoiding disappointment and dealing with the realities of my life. I have often seen people become frustrated or depressed because reality didn't meet with their expectations or desires. I was determined to never allow circumstances to control my behavior or moods. However, I became a little too good at looking at options; in fact, it was so bad that my good friend John Edmunds and brother Jimmy called me "Thous," the man of a thousand ideas. John told this story:

I remember the infamous day when Jimmy and I chose the name "Thous" for Jay. The three of us were on a flight from Las Vegas to Salt Lake City. Jay was sitting behind Jimmy and me. Jay was trying to decide what to do the following weekend and, every few minutes, would pop up from behind the seat and describe a new "option" to us. Finally, Jimmy told him to make up his mind and stay put, because Jimmy was trying to draw a picture of Jay attempting to make up his mind. Jay then said, "I have a thousand options and I can't decide on one!" Jimmy immediately penciled in "thousand options" to his artwork, and history was made—Thous was born!

Individual Identities

My family shared the attitude, "All for one, and one for all," but obviously that could only last for so long. As Donny and Marie started their own businesses, and Jimmy became successful in his new ventures overseas, some of my brothers thought the group as we knew it needed to have a face lift. The "all for one" attitude changed a bit.

Merrill did have quite a bit of a struggle during this time and felt the need to pursue a career on his own without the brothers. Alan felt the need to get involved, financially, and dove into the business side of things. Wayne took off and became a professional pilot. Virl felt the need to be the big brother and hold the family together in a spiritual sense while my parents were on their missions, and this was when my brother Tom began working a "normal" job with the U.S. Postal Service. I was just trying to look at every option I could that would help me to grow and develop both as a person and as a professional.

I grew up with a group identity, and my personal struggle of "finding out who Jay is" began to surface in the late 1970s. I got involved in other things, such as playing football with BYU, and even considered joining the military. But, I could never break away from the fact that I was an Osmond Brother.

Football Fun or Foe?

I was very good at throwing a football, and my brothers encouraged me to try out with BYU. I made the team, though due to our performance schedule, I was never able to play in the actual games—just spring and summer training camps. Football was always a source of relaxation and fun for me, but once I made the team, it felt different. I remember one game where we played against ourselves: the BYU "Blue & White Game" was always played after spring training. I was playing junior varsity at the time. The stands were full, and they were trying out a new quarterback, Mark Giles. Gary Sheide was the quarterback at the time. Gifford Nielsen, Jim McMahon and Mark Wilson were also ready to be tested, and Steve Young had just joined the team. I heard talk about an Osmond playing on the team. I felt pressure to be good because of the comments I was hearing from some people around me as to whether an Osmond could really play or not. So, not only was I trying something that I wasn't confident with, but I also felt I had to prove to myself and to others that an Osmond could play. I kept thinking of my old motto, "Confidence comes from doing," but the fear of failure, my lack of confidence, and not being able to meet up to the expectations of everyone ran in conflict with my desire to just have fun and play football. I remember Coach LaVell Edwards telling me I would be tested at another time along with four other junior varsity quarterbacks. I suddenly realized it wasn't something I wanted, because of the performance anxiety I'd already experienced in show business. I knew then that something I loved so much and had been relaxing and fun could turn into pressure, and I knew I needed to walk away. Even though I regretted that decision many times, I've always been glad for what I learned from the experience. A couple of years later, I organized an intramural team at BYU called "The Nosebleeds," and we ended up being ranked #3 in the whole university. I learned we can do something for fun, be good at it, and not have to take it to a different level—one where we feel we have to prove to others that we are talented or good enough to become "professional." Years later, just for fun, I tried out for the semi-pro football team in Springfield, Missouri—The Springfield Rifles— and made the roster as one of the quarterbacks. It was interesting. I not only wanted to see if I could still play (mid-life crisis), but I also wanted to find out if I still felt the same about the pressure versus having fun. It was through this experience that I learned it is okay to sometimes opt to use our talents for the fun of it, not just vocationally.

In the 1970s, after making the BYU team, our show business agent Stan Moress informed Roman Gabriel (the great quarterback of the Los Angeles Rams) that I made it onto the BYU team. Roman sent a uniform to me that had his number on it, along with an invitation to try out with the Rams. After that BYU Blue & White game, I knew this was something I didn't want to do. Who knows where it would have taken me had I pursued the game?

When I worked on *The Donny & Marie Show,* there were times when our invited guests were NFL greats, such as Fran Tarkenton, Kenny Stabler, Terry Bradshaw, Roger Staubach, and Steve Young. The one I really wanted to throw with refused to throw with me— Joe Namath. He told me he didn't throw for fun; he only threw it for a living.

Utah State Independence

In 1978, I felt I needed some direction but didn't know what I was looking for. I knew I was too dependent on my parents and really didn't know I was "hiding" behind our name. I took a trip with my father to his ranch and, during that time, saw the campus of Utah State University. I knew instantly that I needed to take a break from the studio and find myself. I remember so well how this decision felt like the right thing to do, and it turned out to be one of the best experiences of my life. I got my own apartment, made a lot of friends and lived not as an "Osmond Brother," but as Jay. I felt enlightened, which reconfirmed the fact that there was more to my life than show business, and learned things on another level that would be important to my life. This truly was the first time I experienced a full measure of independence. I went to Utah State during the summer term and fall quarter of 1979, and it was a wonderful turning point in my life. I didn't have to prove anything; I was just me. I'd never been on my own before—and I just loved it. I am glad I listened to those promptings to pursue this venture. This experience at Utah State made a big difference in my perceptions of life and of how I saw myself.

Act 5, Scene 4

THE STUDIO

Before the Osmond Studios in Orem, Utah were built, we were living in Santa Monica, California and all had apartments in the same building, which was owned by our parents. As I mentioned, the decision to build the studio in Utah was brought to a family vote, and Wayne and I really struggled with the whole idea. We had a family voting system at the time—family decisions would be made as a group with majority rule. So, Wayne and I were outvoted on the decision to build the studio. Since our finances were all pulled together as a family, it was a risky and difficult move. Millions were invested into this project. We were later met with many challenges that would tear most families apart. I absolutely feel we were in over our heads with this project, but I also knew it was right. I felt a lot of fear, but for some reason, I knew that whatever was ahead was meant to be.

When the studio was completed, our first thought was, "Oh no! What did we do!?" After our initial panic, we all jumped in and tried to make it work. My job was to represent the studio to producers and directors in Los Angeles. I really enjoyed doing this. Another one of my responsibilities was to make sure the tours for the public were fun and interesting. That was when I met two wonderful people—De Von Tu'ua and Cindy Wankier. De Von was in charge of security, and Cindy oversaw the studio tours. They virtually became family to us. The meaning of family grew much bigger than just our father, mother, and the nine of us. We were expanding in all areas of life.

Another aspect of the studio job I really liked was entertaining the show's guest stars. I really enjoyed making sure our guest stars had a little fun while they were in town. I had a crush on Jaclyn Smith back then, and I remember her secretary asking me if I would mind showing them around Provo. I was more than happy to oblige. I drove them around Provo all day, and the egoboost was great. When David Hasselhoff (who was working on the television show *Knight Rider* at the time) came to town, he reminded me of an old friend of mine, Dave Smith. Dave and I used to run around Provo to meet girls (and is the friend I asked to be the best man at my wedding). I called Dave by the nickname of "Smitty"; and because of David Hasselhoff's resemblance to him, I found I started calling David "Smitty," too. He didn't seem to mind.

Tony Geary was a really cool guy and felt like a brother to me. I couldn't believe how different he was from his character, "Luke Spencer," on *General Hospital.*

Robert Redford would sometimes drop by to see what we were up to at the studio. I really respected his opinion. He lived only a few miles up the canyon from us. I ran into Robert Redford in an airport one time. He said, "Hi Jay!" I honestly didn't know what to call him—Robert, Bob, Mr. Redford. So I responded, "Hi Redford Robert Bob!" He looked at me and said, "Are you ok?!" I told him I was sorry, I had a brain burp. I asked what people call him, and he said his friends call him Bob, so I could call him Bob. He told me he was going to skip the line (this was before high security at the airports) and proceeded to slip behind the airline counter, where they then took him a back way to first class on his flight. I realized I finally had a name for Robert Redford: "Getaway Bob."

Debbie Reynolds was a guest on one of our Osmond family shows, and we became good friends with her. She was just one of the nicest people around. Ann-Margret also made an appearance on one of the Osmond Brothers' specials at our studio (I played drums behind her on one of her songs). She definitely makes the list as one of my favorite celebrities.

Andy Gibb was another wonderful person I got to spend time with during those days. He was a great guy. I remember the many talks about life we had. There was one particular time I remember: He called me on his yacht in Miami, Florida. He was feeling very depressed. He didn't know what to do with himself, so I talked to him until I felt he was feeling more normal. I came to almost feel like a bit of a big brother to him. He seemed so unstable at times and very together at other times. I've always felt as though there might have been something more I could have done for Andy and regret that I didn't do more. It is a tough thing after someone is gone to feel you should have been a better friend.

Our intentions for the studio were good, and it was highly successful for a while. Our desire was for quality productions to come from the studio, but independent productions weren't monitored closely. Our family was not physically available to fully see to the quality control process, and this eventually resulted in the fall of the operation.

The San Diego Disaster

Jimmy and I began playing golf at the Cascade Driving Range where our studio was eventually built. Jimmy and I had some wonderful, fun times playing golf together. Actually, some of the happiest times in my life as a single guy were those spent with my brother Jimmy—playing golf, eating tacos, and singing Paul McCartney songs together. Jimmy became a great golfer, but I struggled with the game, so I felt I needed to get some professional help with it. I went to PGA Hall of Fame Golfer Billy Casper's house for a fireside with Nancy, my girlfriend at the time. I told Billy that I really found a new love for golf, though I wasn't very good at it. Billy and his wife said I should go with them to San Diego to play in a little golf tournament with Johnny Miller—one of the biggest golfers at the time. I again said I wasn't very good, but they insisted it would be fun. They said McLean Stevenson (from M.A.S.H.) and Don Knotts would be there, too. I got to thinking that it would be really fun to fly to San Diego, pick up a few golf tips from Johnny Miller, and meet some fun comedians who probably played the game as poorly as I did, so I agreed to make the trip. I was met at the airport by Ed Barner, who was Johnny Miller's manager at the time. He assured me it would be a very relaxing day of golf. The next day, I went to the country club where the tournament was being played, only to be met with 8,000 screaming Johnny Miller golf fans in attendance. It turned out this "little tournament" was the Celebrity Pro-Am, and I immediately knew I was in way over my head. I was lucky if I could hit the ball, let alone keep up with great golfers like Johnny, Billy, McLean, and Don. Needless to say, you can only imagine my first tee off. Dead silence hung in the air, and I felt panic deep inside as I thought about all of the golf fans that were watching. I'll never forget the trauma I experienced at that moment. I was afraid I was going to kill someone with my bad shots, but I ended up only hitting two people with my golf balls—that wasn't bad! They did have to hire an extra caddy and golf cart to keep looking for my golf ball, though. Don Knotts was really funny and got me through the day. I have to say, I really learned a lot about the game from these golfing greats . . . and also learned what it felt like to jump from the frying pan into the fire.

My blessing day
(*From Left to Right:* Merrill, Father, Alan,
Tom, Virl, me, Mother).

Kindergarten school picture, age 5.

Father holding me outside our home in Ogden, Utah.

Fishing trip in Sweden. I learned to love shrimp.

My third birthday.

Above: Disneyland After Dark performance: Alan, Wayne, Merrill, and me.

Left: One of my favorite pictures as a child.

"Seven Little Foys."

My solo, "Hang on, Sloopy."

Susie and me at a petting zoo in a folk park in Sweden. She wouldn't let go of me!

Our family in Arleta, CA (*From Left to Right:* Alan, Merrill, Mother, Jimmy, Jay, Virl, Marie, Father, Tom, Donny, Wayne).

With my little
buddy, Jimmy.
We spent a lot of
time together.

Right: My beautiful
sister, Marie.

Below: Golfing
with Donny.

Left: From a dance book we once released. Love those bell-bottoms!

Below: With the Dallas Cowboys Cheerleaders when they appeared on our special. My ego was a little out of control!

Left: With Kurt Russell in *The Travels of Jamie McPheeters.*

Below: An early Osmond Brothers publicity photo for Barnaby Records. My brothers just got their brand new Fender guitars.

Football was an important part of my life, too. This uniform was sent to me by Roman Gabriel.

As a quarterback on the BYU Football Team.

At FAME
Studios
in Muscle
Shoals,
Alabama.

Chuck Norris
was our
karate
instructor
and helped us
choreograph
the Karate
segments in
the show.

I used to collect NFL autographs. I received this autographed football shortly after I broke my nose in a karate segment of our show.

A typical scene of Father and Mother (at their home on Mountain Ridge Road in Provo, Utah).

The rehearsal room in our Arleta, CA home: Organizing my new Ludwig drum set.

In the 1970s, I was a representative for Ludwig Drums.

The cover photo from my CD, *It's About Time Again* (2009, taken by Brandon Osmond, Donny's son).

This photo was taken by our longtime friend, Ina Mourik.

Our wedding day, August 25, 1987.

Jimmy told me to get this new outfit for the date I had with Kandi in Burbank back in the Spring of 1987. Good taste?

The entire Osmond family on Oprah (2007).

Meeting Queen
Elizabeth II.

With President Ronald Reagan.

Eric, Marcus, and Jason, Springfield, Missouri (1996 Olin Mills Photography).

Our Family
(*From Left to Right:* Eric, Me, Marcus, Kandi, and Jason.)

Act 6

~1980—1985~

A LITTLE BIT COUNTRY

REINVENTING AND REEXAMINING

The decade of the 1980s was a very different experience for me and my family. It was also very different for the fans that had followed us through the years. It not only was a time of reinventing ourselves, but it was also one of redefining. This stage of our career actually started around 1979 and culminated in 1982. Donny and Marie were going different directions, and Jimmy became more focused on his business ventures. My brother Virl began to pursue his degree (by the way, he was the first of the family to earn a college degree). My brother Tom was working with the U.S. Postal Service; and Alan, Wayne, Merrill, and I reverted back to our deep roots of singing harmony. Country music seemed to be a natural step forward for us. However, I found the country music thing a bit confining. I didn't really feel comfortable in this genre. Even though we recorded a few albums and dressed the part, being "country" just wasn't me. I was a rocker at heart! I knew where my heart was musically, but my brothers and I decided we wanted to give country music a try, especially since Conway Twitty talked us into singing backup for him on the hit, "Heartache Tonight." After a few years, it seemed to me that it just wasn't the right path for us in the entertainment business.

This period of time was very difficult for our family. We had a barrage of financial disasters. It was like a big spiral downward. It wasn't just the bad advice we were given; but as a family, we were caught up in a world of luxury and materialism. We had everything anyone could ever want. We owned several expensive cars. I had a Mercedes 450 SL and a Rolls Royce. Wayne had a 182 Skylane single-engine airplane and a twin-engine Cessna 210. We also had a family prop-jet plane we called "The Blue Goose," which was big and scary for me to fly in. We owned two speed boats, several motorcycles, snowmobiles, and a host of other things. We built mansions in Utah on a cul-de-sac which the city named "Osmond Lane." Our net worth was between $40,000,000–$80,000,000 (no one really could account exactly how much). However, in my opinion, we were unwise stewards, because we let others take hold of our finances and control our money. The investments my parents wisely made were what ended up saving us from bankruptcy.

During this tough time, so many people told our father to "Sue, sue, sue"; his response was, "No, no, no!" He said we needed to look at ourselves, take responsibility, and "learn, learn, learn." I could always count on my father to do the right thing— he was a great example of integrity.

In the midst of all of this chaos, my parents managed to keep us all together, and eventually the debts were worked out. They handled the financial trauma we found ourselves in with dignity and integrity. What would have shattered some families strengthened ours.

Money can be a blessing or a curse, and it had become a curse for us. I personally believe we were focusing too much on "things" and "money," so the Lord took it away from us. I look back and feel grateful in a strange way that He did. It seemed like overnight that we lost it all. Our storage sheds, which were full of priceless items and personal family treasures, were even looted.

I learned some of my greatest lessons during this time. I learned that "things" don't matter after awhile. I also learned the truthfulness of the words from my friend Derek Spriggs: "Money brings comforts—not happiness." These words of wisdom have always stayed with me.

Getting to Know My Father

I used to hate horses because I carried the memory with me of my grandfather being killed by one. When I was in my late twenties, my father bought a ranch in Avon, Utah. He had about 200 head of cattle and quite a few horses. He was excited about the ranch and wanted me to experience "ranching" first-hand. I wasn't into the great outdoors but thought this would be a good time to get to know my father better.

This is when I became close to my father. We had some wonderful times at that ranch. We talked and rode horses. He taught me how to herd and brand cattle, and how to barrel race. I remember this one particular night after we had been out herding cattle, we were totally exhausted from the day. That night, I had a nightmare that I was herding cattle. My father told me that I picked up a pillow and hurled it around my head, swinging and knocking things over. I then ended up chasing him down the hall, screaming, "You stupid cow!" We had some great laughs about it the next day. I realize how many years I missed not knowing this side of my father, and what a "marshmallow" he really was. My father had a hardcore outer shell—stern, but loving—and I'd always felt a little afraid of him. That is, until I spent these wonderful times at the ranch with him. These are some of my best memories of my father—when I lost that fear of him and he became my buddy.

Uncle Rulon and the Break-In

Uncle Rulon, who was a lot like my father, was staying with us at our house on Mountain Ridge in Provo, Utah. My father loved Uncle Rulon, and they were very close. In fact, I've always tried to model my relationships with my brothers by their example. I was working for the studio at that time and was flying quite often to Los Angeles representing Osmond Studios. On one particular day, as I was leaving the house, I remember telling Uncle Rulon, "Please be sure to push this button and set the alarm when you leave." When he left, he thought he followed those directions correctly. About two hours later, I received a call that the alarm had gone off and there were four police cars at the house. I hurried back as the police were searching the house. Their report read, "Bedroom ransacked." I was too embarrassed to tell them that was just the way I kept my room, so I went along with the report.

Wyoming Cookies

We had a performance in Casper, Wyoming, and the trip was long and boring. We were in a bus and got off the highway to go into a gas station to get some treats. I saw some oval-shaped dog biscuits and thought, "What a great idea! I'll give these to everyone on the bus and see how long they can handle them!" I got on the bus and told everyone I had some sugarless cookies that were absolutely fantastic. Sam Foster thought they tasted like dust. Brook Langton loved them and must have eaten ten of them. Some of the family liked them, too. After everyone had eaten most of the cookies, I showed them the package. Ron Clark ordered the bus to stop. They made me get off the bus in the middle of nothingness in Wyoming, and took off. I stood there with my suitcase and a strange feeling of desertion. They did come back—about 15 minutes later. I gratefully got back on the bus. I always wondered, was that hint of dog breath coming from inside the bus just my imagination?

COUNTRY IDENTITY?

During the 1980s, the Osmond Brothers were searching for our niche in the industry. Obviously, we wanted to try to make our mark in country music, but we eventually started drifting back to pop and rock. I guess it could be said that, as a group, we are unclassifiable. Variety has always been our forte. Perhaps that is what has given us our staying power in this business: we strive to reach audiences of all ages and tastes in music.

After working together as producers of *The Donny & Marie Show*, I felt the dynamics of the brothers changed. Different traits and talents were brought out after those five years of working on the show. Merrill was more of a "wheeler/dealer" and wanted to go on his own. Alan became known as "bizarre-o," because his creativity was beyond everyone else's. Wayne became a great songwriter and more of a hermit; and then there was me. I just had enough! I was determined to go back to school and live a "normal" life, but that didn't last long.

Christmas in Washington

In 1984, we performed in the special "Christmas in Washington" with President Reagan. I sat behind the President as he gave his speech. I had a crick in my neck, and apparently the President had one in his, too, because we both displayed the same twitch. If you watch closely, you'll think I was purposely mimicking his twitch. My boys get such a kick out of that when they watch the video. Ronald Reagan loved our family, and we had a great respect for him. We were honored to have been invited to appear in that special with President and Mrs. Reagan.

Our Parents' Missions

Our parents went on two missions for The Church of Jesus Christ of Latter-day Saints. The first one was to Hawaii in 1981, and the second followed directly after that to London, England in 1984. They served as directors at the LDS visitor centers. I remember spending Christmas of 1984 with them in London and have fond memories of going to Harrod's to buy a little Christmas tree for them. They devoted their entire lives to the Lord—what great examples for me. I asked my father one time what made him feel he wanted to go on a mission. This is when he discussed his thoughts about refinement with me. He wanted to "refine" instead of "retire." By going on a mission, he was dedicating his life to refinement and serving. My parents were reinventing and redefining themselves, as well. What a wonderful way to use that time of their lives.

When they returned from their missions, Mother and Father joined us in Branson, Missouri. Our father used to help people get on and off the motor coaches that visited The Osmond Family Theater. They would come to our shows and spend time talking with people who saw us perform. Mother would take time to visit with fans and answer questions they had about our family . . . and life in general. Everyone loved it when Father and Mother came by the theater.

Starting Over, Financially

I think of all the decades, the 1980s held the most growth, as well as the most pain. I feel this is true not only for Alan, Wayne,

Merrill, and myself, but for Donny, Marie, and Jimmy, as well. Our older brothers, Virl and Tom, also stretched as they tried to find themselves.

As a singing group, this was the turning point of our music careers. It forced us all to take a good look at how we were viewed by our audiences. Financially, we had to start over. At this point, I felt Alan, Wayne, Merrill, and I were in the best shape, physically, but in the worst shape, professionally and financially.

TIME FOR A CHANGE

In 1981, we finished a world tour with the final concert held at the Marriott Center in Provo, Utah. I thought this would be one of our last big shows we performed as a family. Our interests and desires had become very diverse. Our parents had been called on their missions, Virl and Tom went into business for themselves, the brothers were giving country music a try, Donny got involved in theater, Marie was pursuing her country music career, and Jimmy was becoming very successful in business and acting. I wanted to travel some more and continue with my studies. I even became engaged to Miss BYU, Teresa Chingas (though it turned out neither of us was ready to be married). The 1970s were like a whirlwind, but the 1980s were more like a hurricane—we were pulled apart as an entertainment family.

Marriott Grilling

I was back in the dating scene and wondering what I was really looking for in a girl. I really didn't know at the time. All I did know was that there were too many girls! How could someone settle down with an attitude like that? So, I tried really hard to focus on being more serious.

One time, J. Willard and Bill Marriott, along with their wives, called me in to the office at their hotel for a chat, because I was dating Bill's daughter, Debbie. They proceeded to grill me, asking questions about why I wanted to date Debbie, what my thoughts were on marriage, where I was in my educational pursuit, and what kind of man I was. I was very impressed with their questioning, but it really put me on the spot. They didn't realize I was also dating other girls besides Debbie. This particular meeting began the pressure I would feel later on in life to get married. I really liked Debbie and thought she was a cool girl; but, I wasn't ready to settle down knowing my heart was also with other girls. I will forever be grateful for that day, though, because it made me think more seriously about getting married.

This started what I referred to as "the Symptoms of Single Life." In my mind, there were five symptoms: (1) mental anxiety—whom should I marry, what should I look for in a girl, will I find the right girl soon, what if I don't, etc.; (2) physical frustration—I was a "player," but I managed to stay true to my morals; (3) social pressure—why I wasn't married, what was holding me back, I wasn't getting any younger, etc.; (4) spiritual stagnation—I felt I wasn't moving along with the Lord's program; and (5) emotional emptiness. I went home time after time following a date and felt lonely that there wasn't anyone with whom I could share my experiences and to whom I could have a long-term commitment. Being aware of these symptoms told me that I was starting the process of becoming ready for marriage.

Living the Normal Life

Once again, I found I was becoming curious about living the "normal life." I would question my friends about their jobs and nine-to-five lifestyles. I was determined to find peace in that pursuit. In 1985, I decided to leave the only life I ever really knew and try to discover who I was as an individual. I remember having the same sort of feeling when I went to Logan, Utah, in 1979 when I attended Utah State University. However, this time I was going out on my own, and I really believed that I would not go back to show business.

I could have let family pressures keep me from doing what I knew in my heart I had to do, but my parents were supportive of my decision. Wayne, Merrill, and especially Alan were not as supportive; in fact, they were angry with me. The Osmond Brothers went on without me. My brother Jimmy was my biggest supporter, and that helped me to do what I really felt I needed to at that stage of my life.

At first, it didn't really bother me that my brothers continued entertaining without me, but there was always that sense of comfort when I worked with them, and that was now missing from my life.

I had mixed feelings of fear and excitement about what lay ahead for me. The biggest part of me though, was excited to start this new adventure on my own.

I found an apartment in Murray, Utah, and I thought it felt great. I was *just Jay* for three months. I hardly did anything but think, pray, and ponder my life. Then one night when I was out on a date, I felt a hand grab my arm. It was an old friend of mine, Robert Spencer, who was the Dean of Admissions and Records at Brigham Young University. I can remember him saying, "Jay, I've been looking for you for three months! Where have you been? No one has your number, and I almost gave up on you." This came as a big shock; I hadn't realized I'd basically been *hiding* for three months. The only places I went during this time were to the grocery store and church. Robert said, "I have a job offer for you. I know it sounds crazy, but you keep coming into my mind."

I had made plans to move to Los Angeles and work with a public relations firm. I was planning on a life in California in public relations partly because that was an area I had some experience in from my career in entertainment. I also wanted to go to California, because in Utah there were so many Mormon girls that I was becoming obsessed with dating and looked compulsively for the girl who would be right for me. I was trying way too hard and felt that California would limit my options, therefore making it easier to find "her." However, after talking with my friend and Dean of BYU, something made me consider the offer he made to me. I believe that anyone who is praying for guidance will receive it, though we must also study all options before making a decision. God will then lead us to what is best. We can't expect the Lord to guide our footsteps if we are not willing to move our feet. I knew that sitting in my apartment would not get me where I needed to be, and I had to start moving and put a plan together.

Act 6, Scene 4

SO LONG, FAREWELL

I took the position of Admissions Representative at BYU in 1985; and while working in this position, I met Kandilyn Harris. I didn't have to go to California to find the right girl for me after all. Ironically, the "right girl" was from California.

My decision to leave the field of entertainment and operate in a different world that was so foreign gave me a completely different life experience that I wouldn't have otherwise had. I know it broadened my view of things—of people and life. I know one of the greatest things I took from that stage of my life was meeting my sweet wife, Kandilyn.

BYU Recruiting

I started working at BYU in 1985 in the recruiting office and as a spokesperson for the university. This was a big challenge for me, because I had to commit for at least a year and participate in the admitting and denying process of students at BYU. After a year, I began working in a counseling position. By that time, I somehow knew I had fulfilled what I set out to do. The hardest part of my work at BYU was dealing with disappointed parents of admissions candidates—especially the mothers. It was my job to defuse angry parents and defend the committee's decisions as to who was admitted and who wasn't. I would take many cases back to the committee for review but often had the ultimate task of telling parents their son or daughter would not be admitted.

The work day structure was one that I actually loved. After so many years of traveling, interviews, concerts, taping and recording, etc., the daily structure seemed to give me a balance that I needed. I believe it was about a year later that Alan, Wayne, and Merrill stopped performing as a group and focused on individual projects.

The hardest part for me at this stage was finding my identity. I wanted to be Jay but had a lot of people bring up the "Osmond thing." The Dean and I even discussed the idea of changing my last name. When I first started at BYU, I felt like a porcupine in a balloon factory. I started to adjust and eventually settled into the groove of an admissions counselor. The performing side of me, however, was just too strong. That is why, several years later, when Jimmy brought the opportunity to work in Branson at our own theater, it just felt right to perform again with my brothers. I also knew that I would never really be able to get away from the stigma of being an Osmond.

A Drumming Opportunity Forgotten

During the 1970s, the teen magazine *Flip* named me one of the top drummers in the country. I was very flattered by this and thought how nice it was to be singled out for doing something that I love.

In the 1980s, I received several opportunities to go out on my own in show business. I received an offer from CMN (The Children's Miracle Network) to host a show in 1984. I turned everything down, because doing something on my own in the business I was trying to escape from didn't appeal to me at the time. One of my regrets, though, was passing up an offer from famed music director, Mike Post. Mike liked my drumming a lot and told me if I went to Los Angeles, he'd make me his drummer for his projects. It reminded me of the opportunity I had to be a quarterback: I knew I could do it, but I didn't know if that was what I really wanted to do. I could have gone to L.A. and become like the drummers who were my idols: Jimmy Gordon, Ronnie Tutt, Johnny Garin, and Hal Blaine. Just a few weeks before Karen Carpenter died, we went to see her and her brother Richard at the Convention Center in Anaheim, California. We were planning on recording a Christmas album with them. Karen, The Carpenters' drummer Hal Blaine, and I were representatives for Ludwig Drums. It was Hal Blaine who motivated me to eventually record "Topsy," which I released on both of my solo recordings, *It's About Time* and *It's About Time Again.* Many of the drum riffs I play on "Topsy" were from Hal's recording of the song back in the 1960s. Johnny Garin was a session drummer who played on some of our songs, and I really liked his style (several things in my drum solo are included as a result of studying his technique). Jimmy Gordon was my first drum teacher; he was one of Andy Williams' drummers. I used to try to mimic Jimmy's style; and he'd tell me that rather than trying to do just what he taught me, I needed to do my own thing. He told me to take the best I could from him, John, and Ronnie and develop my own style. I took his advice, and that is precisely what I did. I always dreamed of being a hugely successful session drummer like him. My mother always said, "Prepare yourself and the opportunity will come." I did prepare, and the opportunity came. But, did I want to leave the family to become a studio session drummer? I chose not to go for it and decided to go to college, instead. It is interesting to think about where Mike Post's offer might have taken me.

I've since learned that Rick Allen, drummer from Def Leppard, said he was an Osmond fan and respected my drumming. Billy Mason, drummer for Tim McGraw, told me that he was influenced by my drumming, as well. It is nice to know that my drumming has had an impact on others, just as other drummers have had an impact on me.

Act 7

~1986—1990~

A WHOLE NEW LIFE

THE FLIP SIDE OF MY LIFE

I worked at BYU as an admissions counselor from 1986–1990. In addition to being an admissions counselor, I also oversaw 15 employees and approximately eight part-time students in the Admissions Processing Department as the processing manager. I thought the Dean was joking when he put me in charge of all of these people, because they knew a heck of a lot more about the job than I did. I accepted the challenge, though, and went for it. It was very humbling to work my way through the bottlenecks of processing and to try to keep everyone happy at the same time. I knew the Dean put me through the paces not only because he knew I was capable, but he believed I could bring a different perspective to the whole operation. I was shocked that he had such confidence in me, and it really made me feel good about myself—even though I was winging it big time.

Those who know me know I have zero skills in office work; but because the Dean trusted me, I linked a bridge. He knew I was willing to take on this challenge, and I really grew as a result. To some people, fear is an indication to back off, and to some extent fear is good. I believe we experience both rational and irrational fears. What I felt while working at BYU encompassed a little of both.

Jeff Tanner, the Associate Dean of Admissions and Records, didn't like me at first and didn't buy into the Dean's confidence in me. Jeff was distant but very professional—he did everything by the book. He later admitted, after we became friends, that he thought the Dean had lost his mind when I was given the job at BYU. They had interviewed at least 40 very capable people for the position. Jeff was very leery about me that first year. As time moved on, he saw I caught on and was doing well. Jeff could tell that I was sincerely interested in being a team player, and it was obvious I was genuinely interested in helping people. He told me that my desire to work hard and do my best really paid off. Jeff began to trust me and even listened to my opinions. By the end of my four years at BYU, not only had Jeff confided in me about his own challenges, but we also became trusted friends.

In addition to the impact Jeff Tanner had on my experience with BYU, there were several other people there that greatly affected my life. George Vaieland was the head counselor who worked with me. He was an amazing mentor for me in my position of admissions counselor. Norm Finlinson was my colleague who worked with the Dean at BYU and later became the Dean, himself. I have a deep respect for this man; he taught me about the purpose of having values and staying true to them. There were so many other people I learned to love and respect there: Raylene Hadley, Kirk Strong, Tom Gourley (who was very helpful in my training for school relations), Rex Pugmire, Gene Pridey, Pat Williams, Dennis Black, Derek Spriggs, Mary Beth Weston, Erlend Peterson, Scott Ferrin, Scott Ferguson, and so many others were honorable, good, solid people who blessed my life.

In 1986, the Barbershop Harmony Society's Convention was held in Salt Lake City, Utah. I was no longer in show business, but my brothers and I were invited to sing at the convention. I just couldn't turn down this opportunity. When we were kids, we were voted the most likely to become barbershop champs in the future. During this 1986 convention, we were made honorary champs and lifetime members of the Barbershop Harmony Society, legally and historically named the Society for the Preservation and Encouragement of Barber Shop Quartet Singing in America, Inc. (SPEBSQSA). Singing barbershop style with my brothers again took me back to our roots, and it really felt great. This event planted a little seed in the back of my mind that would soon grow to be a reminder of how much I missed doing what I know best— entertaining.

ALONG CAME KANDI

At one point, my assignment was to get the admissions process-ing to work in a smoother way; study the bottlenecks in the system; and report them to the Dean. It was during that time that I met Kandilyn. My personal life was a bit scattered. I was dat-ing a lot of girls, and I even had a list of girls that I wanted to date.

I remember sitting on a table, talking with some colleagues, and telling them that I decided to focus on just the girls on my list (there were about 40 of them). I said I was not going to take on any more names, because I really needed to get serious about getting married. Just then, a cute little blonde gal walked up to the admissions office window. It was as if someone had pushed me off the table. I jumped from the table to the applications window and introduced myself. I remember hearing my friends laughing behind me, because my resolve to not get anymore girls' names flew right out the window . . . and into that admissions window. I had to get her name!

My "car salesman" approach didn't work very well with Kandilyn. In fact, it turned her off so much that she became angry and considered putting in a complaint about me. I managed to get her name, anyway, and checked out her classes. No, I wasn't stalking her, but I did find my access to her schedule a convenient way to "bump into her." Each time I did, however, I got the cold shoulder. I was finally about to give up on her, but for some reason she started being nice to me. On one occasion, I remember mumbling something like, "Maybe we can get together sometime?" I was pleasantly surprised when she agreed. Knowing what a sweet and genuine person Kandilyn is, it seems funny when I think back on those rough times she gave me all those years ago. Kandi describes our dating experience this way:

It was the second block of the fall semester of 1986 at Brigham Young University. I was not quite 20 years old and had arrived in Provo, Utah halfway through the term due to an unexpected foot surgery that had put a halt to my dancing aspirations and caused me to miss a whole two months of the life I loved. It was a life filled with studying and socializing; early-morning cram sessions and late-night flirting. It was a world that I had happily anticipated returning to for my junior year after a long and comparatively uneventful summer working in California as a typist/clerk for the Burbank Unified School District. It had been great to be able to spend some time at home with my family, to see old friends, and to build up my bank account; but I couldn't wait to get back, and having to spend weeks in a cast instead of where I wanted to be put me in an uncharacteristically bad mood. The weeks of waiting for my foot to heal passed slowly.

Finally the day arrived. After arriving back at the "Y," I found myself happily settled into my new apartment with my old friends. It felt so good to be back, yet I found myself having to move at a fast pace. It was the morning of November 12, and I was running behind. I was running behind academically (the block term went twice as fast as a semester); socially (although I was with some of my roommates from the previous years, everyone else in the apartment complex already seemed to know each other, and I felt left out); and literally (I was late getting out the door to begin my day). That's when the phone rang. It was my mom calling from California. It was her second call in a week and that was unusual. I wondered what was wrong. "Did you send that application to me yet for Rob?" My younger brother planned to attend BYU the following year, and my mom had that "worried mom" sound in her voice. "Yes, Mom, I sent it a week ago." "Well it hasn't arrived, and I'm worried that if we don't get his application filled out and sent in immediately he won't get into BYU. Please go pick up another application and get it mailed TODAY!" She was now using her motherly authoritarian voice, the one my 19-year-old self dared not argue with. "Yes Mom, I promise I'll get another application in the mail today."

Normally, I'm a very amiable person. Characteristically, I'm a person who is generally well liked and pleasant to be around. But this wasn't a normal day. Months of frustration had built up. Time was short and money wasn't plentiful. These were the days of cold cereal and bean burritos, the days when having to spend a couple extra bucks to mail a piece of paper that I had already paid to mail the previous week (and having to do it on a day that I was already overloaded) was putting me into my quick and efficient mode. This is the kind of mood when I'm not terribly patient and people who know me well know to get out of my way. I was in a "let's just get this done and don't mess with me" attitude. That was the day I first met Jay Osmond.

I entered the administration building at the north end of campus for the second time that week. I walked quickly to the admissions window where I knew I would be handed a brand new application form the moment I asked for it. I anticipated grabbing the form, hurrying to the post office, and putting it in the mail before my first class that day. Well, my plan was not to be.

Arriving at the admissions window, I found that no one working there came to help me the way they did on my previous visit. All of the employees were either on the phone or helping other students. In exactly the same way that it seems traffic lights are always red when you're hurrying to drive to an appointment on time, so it was at the window that day. Even though it was no one's fault, I couldn't seem to get any help. All I needed was to be handed an application form, and I would be on my merry way.

Just as I was anticipating climbing over the counter and finding the form for myself, a nice-looking man in his late twenties/early thirties (and looking very official in a suit and tie) moved from the back of the room and approached the counter. "I don't really work in this department, but can I help you with something?" he politely asked. "Yes, thank you, I just need an application form," I said, looking at the piles of papers behind him. "Is it for you or are you already a student here?" he asked. "I'm a student. It's for my brother who plans to apply for next year." "Where does your brother live?" he asked. Thinking this was an odd question, but wanting to hurry out the door, I answered, "Burbank, California." "And what is his name?" he asked. Thinking this was another unnecessary question, I curtly answered, "Rob Harris." With a big smile he then asked, "And what is your name?" This guy was flirting with me! Not only was he much too old for me, but he was a BYU Administrator, and I didn't think he should be coming on to me. Besides, by this time, I was really running late. I wasn't going to make it to the post office on time without missing my class. Through gritted teeth I grudgingly answered, "Kandi." He finally handed me the application and said something cheesy like, "I hope your brother enjoys BYU." I managed a strained smile, took the paper, and stormed out of the building.

Walking as fast as I could, angry thoughts were flying through my mind. How dare that guy ask me all those personal questions? He had no right! He doesn't need to know all that information in order to hand me an application! You should march right back in there and demand to know HIS name, HIS student status, and where HE'S from! That guy was so presumptuous! He thought he could get away with that behavior with that great big smile of his! I felt very irked. He really got under my skin at our first meeting, and it definitely made for a memorable moment.

It wasn't until the second time we met that I found out his name. When he told me he was Jay Osmond, I said, "Oh, do you mean like Donny and Marie?" He said, "Yes, I'm their brother." I wasn't sure he was telling me the truth, so I looked at his teeth (because I heard that Osmonds had nice teeth). His teeth looked great, so I figured he must be telling the truth. I didn't know about the Osmond Brothers, just Donny and Marie, because I watched their show when I was a kid.

I thought he was a really nice guy, but I wasn't interested in dating an entertainer. Having grown up in Burbank, California, I knew a lot of people in show business; unfortunately, the experience had not always been positive. I was hoping to meet a nice, normal guy with a normal job and a normal lifestyle. I wanted to meet a returned missionary, an Eagle Scout, and either a pre-med or pre-law student who was just a few years older than me. Boy, was I ever wrong about that!

Jay kept showing up wherever I went. I thought it was odd that he not only attended my church meetings on Sunday, but also came to my dance class later that week. Each time we ran into each other he would ask me out. I just wasn't comfortable with the idea and was honestly very busy, so I kept saying no. After about four months of this, I got my weekly phone call from my mom one day. She was asking her usual questions. "How is school?" "How are your roommates?" "Are you dating anyone special?" When I mentioned Jay, she seemed apprehensive. I guess the idea of a 32-year-old guy taking out your 20-year-old daughter will do that to a mom. But then I told her his last name. "Osmond? As in THE Osmonds?" she said. "What's he like? Is he nice?" I said, "Yes, he's really nice." "Well, then, why don't you go out with him once. It could be a journal entry." I said, "All right, if he asks me again, I will." A couple of days later, he did ask me out again and I said yes. I will always owe a debt of gratitude to my insightful mother!

Our first date was to dinner at a place called "Chi-Chis," a Mexican restaurant in Provo. I remember being very impressed with Jay. He wasn't at all like I thought he would be. He was so kind, humble, gracious, thoughtful, and interesting. I remember just feeling so great being with him. That night in my journal I wrote what a great person I thought he was and that I would feel honored if he would even consider me to be his friend. By our second date I was in love. If he had proposed marriage at that moment, I would have said yes.

The first two months we dated we saw each other about once a week. In April, I went home during the Spring/Summer term to work at my job as a secretary at the Burbank Unified School District, while Jay was still working at BYU. About once every week or so, from April until August, either Jay flew to California to see me, or I flew to Utah to see him. Our typical dates in the beginning involved going out to dinner and seeing a movie.

The first members of Jay's family I met were his parents. He brought them to a dance class I was taking. I had long hair at the time and often wore it in an inside-out French braid (because I couldn't do it right-side out). Jay's mother noticed it that night and referred to me as "the girl with the pretty French braid," until Jay and I got more serious. Jay was dating so many girls, I wasn't surprised. I thought his parents were an extremely nice couple.

On our third date, Jay and I had dinner at his sister Marie's house. I was so nervous I could hardly eat or talk. I had two reasons to be so nervous. The obvious reason is that I was meeting Marie Osmond, whom I had admired since I was a little girl. The other reason was that earlier that day, Jay kissed me for the first time, and I was entering a relationship that would change my life forever. I also met Jimmy earlier that day and think it was about that same time that I met Donny. I didn't meet the rest of Jay's family until the first few weeks we were married, though Jay had each of his other brothers call me in California to say hello before our wedding day.

In 1986, I moved from my apartment in Salt Lake City to live with my parents in Pleasant Grove, Utah. Every morning I would take a little walk with my mother for about half an hour; then she would fix some hot chocolate for me and we'd spend time talking before I went to work at BYU. This time was priceless to me.

One night, I came home very late but had to go upstairs and talk to my parents. I told my mother there was something special about Kandilyn, and I couldn't get her out of my head. My father, who supposedly was sleeping, sat up and said, "Jay, if you don't ask that girl to marry you, I will ask her for you!" I said, "You're right!" I made what seemed like a long walk down the hallway to the phone. I knew what I was about to do was the right thing, but I was really nervous. I think it was 11:00 P.M. her time in California. I was going to pop the question and felt sure she would say "yes." I was concerned, however, about the timing of my proposal. I knew Kandi had a problem with the whole Osmond-showbiz thing, and she also had some personal plans that I knew were important to her. She was contemplating joining the BYU Ballroom Dance Team and was also considering going on a mission for the church.

I made the call. Kandi's dad answered the phone. I cleared my throat and told Clint Harris I would love to marry his daughter. I asked him if she said "yes," would it be all right with him? He nicely said, "I think that is up to her." Kandi's dad handed the phone to Kandi; and trying to be witty I said, "Is this who I think it is?" She had a crack in her voice, and somehow I lost my confidence. I said, "I've been thinking, and I would really love to marry you!" Kandi screamed into the phone. Remembering she once told me when it came time for her to marry someone, she would want to make sure to pray about it before she gave her answer. So I said, "I want you to think about this and pray about it. If your answer is "no," we can continue to date. I could go under the name of Jason Wesley, so the Osmond thing wouldn't be a problem, or we can wait a while so you can be on the dance team. Or, you can go on a mission, and we can wait and see how we feel afterwards." There was a pause on the other end of the phone, and then Kandi said, "Okay, I will let you know tomorrow when you come to see me."

I was sure Kandi would rethink that initial scream and instead take me up on one of the options I offered; so rather than make the trip to see her, I sent two dozen red roses and gave her a call the next night. Kandi was really upset with me; she had bought a brand new dress and was waiting to see me. So, the next day I flew to Burbank. Kandi met me at the airport and was really in a daze.

She even forgot where she parked her car, and we spent an hour looking for it (this was before the handy key fobs we now have). Finally, Kandi let me know all of those options were not an option. I was a very lucky guy—she said "yes!"

The next few months were a blur for me. Wedding preparations took a large chunk of our time, but it was well worth it. Kandi describes our wedding this way:

> Our wedding took place in the Salt Lake Temple in Salt Lake City, Utah. My parents, as well as his, were married there, so there was no question of where the wedding would take place. It was a Tuesday afternoon. I remember feeling unusually calm. I arrived at the temple with my parents. I remember I wore a dark blue dress with a white lace collar, and my mom carried my wedding dress.
>
> The ceremony was beautiful and emotional. All of our family members on each side were there. Afterward, we gathered outside the temple to take photos. I remember Jay kept twitching his neck. I didn't realize until later how nervous he was.
>
> After the photos, we took two horse-drawn carriages from Temple Square to the Marriott Hotel for our reception. Jay and I were in one carriage with my parents, and Jay's parents rode in the other carriage with my two grandmothers, Rose Harris and Evelyn Holmstead.
>
> At the hotel we took even more photos and then stood in a line with our two sets of parents to greet our guests. We had over 3,000 people attend the reception. I felt so bad we weren't able to talk longer to each guest who stood in the huge line to greet us. We both have large, extended families that we are close to—plus Jay invited practically everyone he'd ever met. I think he wanted undeniable proof that he was actually, finally, getting married.

For our honeymoon, we went to Amsterdam and London. Once we returned home, we lived at Jay's apartment in Salt Lake City for the final few days of his lease. Then, we stayed at the Comfort Inn in Provo until we could move into our house. This was just the beginning of a whole new world for me.

I'm grateful for the path my life took, which led to my meeting Kandilyn. I believe everything happens for a reason and really believe that we were led to each other. I dated a lot of wonderful girls, but I believe when people are ready to get married and they are prayerful about it, the Lord will lead them to the right person.

THE VOID FROM NOT BEING "AN OSMOND"

After Kandi and I were married, and just before our first child was born, I discovered there was a void I hadn't quite put my finger on until this stage of my life. I read in the newspaper one day that my three brothers, Alan, Wayne, and Merrill (who had gotten back together as a group) were going to be performing at the Utah State Fair—without me! I had a very strange feeling come over me as I read this news. I was living in Provo, Utah, and was still considered a "newlywed." I was working at BYU as a counselor and had a whole different life from that of my brothers. However, reality (or more like "identity") hit me hard. I had a terrible feeling of anxiety at the thought of going to their show as a spectator. I remember when my brothers entered the stage, my heart jumped, and I had a feeling inside of me as though I was late for my queue. Watching the show, I was thinking, *Wayne is really funny, and the sound is good, though it is missing a vocal part, and it needs a drum solo. Oh . . . that is because I'm here in the audience instead of on stage with my brothers.*

Being at an Osmond Brothers performance was a first for Kandilyn. I was talking a lot during the performance, just trying to explain to her what it was like to perform as an Osmond, as a myriad of other things were spinning through my mind.

During the show, my brothers invited me on stage to sing a number with them. When I heard the audience's reaction to my joining my brothers on stage, I realized how much I missed that. It felt like putting on a pair of old shoes (that's "shoe business"). The only way I can describe it is that it was like riding a bike—it was just very natural. It wasn't until that moment that I realized how much I missed feeling comfortable with what I was doing; and, I also realized at that moment how my decision to move on had its consequences. It was there, that night, that I knew I had to somehow find my way back into the comfort zone of working with my brothers—the group that I knew I was meant to be part of.

I only sang two songs with my brothers that night, and did a drum solo. I think the songs were "Old Man Auctioneer" and "I Think About Your Lovin'." I can't recall which song I played my drum solo to. It went like clockwork. There was energy in the air and in the audience. A girl in the crowd screamed and gave me a big hug and kiss as I returned to my seat after the two songs. Kandilyn was surprised by this. Remember, this was her first real experience with an Osmond Brothers' live performance.

Kandi had never seen an Osmond concert, let alone seen me get up on stage and go to work. Then, for me to get kissed by a stranger in the audience—what a shock! She thought she married an admissions officer who worked at BYU. I think it was the experience at this concert that set the stage for my decision to go to Branson, Missouri when Jimmy presented that offer a few years later.

The next day at work in the office at BYU, I knew things weren't going to be the same for me. I was aware that my job there would eventually come to an end and that my future would be back with my brothers. I was torn, because I had come to love the people I worked with at BYU and the structured lifestyle I was living. I knew, however, that my brothers missed me, and I missed them, too.

JASON GEORGE OSMOND

Jason came along on September 23, 1988—13 months after Kandilyn and I were married. Actually, at the beginning of our marriage, I was hesitant to have children right away. Just as with the idea of marriage, I was actually scared to death to be a father. But, it wasn't long before I knew I was ready to take a leap of faith; and together, Kandilyn and I knew it was time to start a family.

I remember so vividly that very special morning when Kandilyn came into my office at BYU. I was standing behind my desk, and she came in and closed the door. She said, "I have something wonderful to tell you!" I asked her what it was, and she said, "I'm pregnant!" I fell to my chair in shock and felt an indescribable joy.

Growing up, I obviously had a lot of wonderful nephews and nieces. I really loved kids, but I didn't think I would be a great dad. This feeling concerned me until the day that "fatherly love" took hold of my heart, and it has never let go. I remember so clearly the day I looked at the little bump on Kandi's tummy. I tapped on her tummy, and there was a little tap back. I was never the same after that moment. I completely fell in love with the idea of having children. I can't see a child anymore without thinking,

"That's someone's Jason, Eric, or Marcus." Children teach us things we need to learn, just as much as we teach them.

Part of me was relieved that we were on our way to parenthood, and part of me felt very anxious about becoming a parent. There was no question, though, that my life was taking a turn that I would never regret. Kandi explains it this way:

> We suspected and really hoped that I was pregnant. After visiting the doctor and getting confirmation, I drove to Jay's office to give him the exciting news. At first he was ecstatic—then he turned pale and I thought he was going to faint. I had to get him a chair so he could sit down for a moment. Once he recovered, he took me around to all of his associates in the building to tell them the happy news.
>
> We were both so happy, we could hardly contain ourselves. We bought a book called, *What to Expect When You're Expecting,* and read it over and over. It was our go-to book. I was the first to get married and get pregnant of all of my close friends, my mom lived in California, and I wasn't really close to Jay's mother — yet. I remember feeling very alone as I became more and more sick. I was so weak, because I was sick the whole nine months and had to go on IV fluids just to survive. It was an extremely difficult time for me and for Jay. We went through it hand-in-hand, every step of the way. We always knew the outcome would be worth it, and was it ever! We got our Jason!
>
> Jay was with me when I gave birth. We filmed the experience, and Jay even got to cut the umbilical cord. Jason was born at the UVRMC in Provo, Utah. Jay decided on Jason's name years before we ever met. He basically said, "Will you marry me? Our first son's name will be Jason George Osmond." Well, not exactly, but it was a name that Jay really wanted to use. His nickname used to be Jason, and he had asked all of his

brothers to please not use the name for their children, so he could. Luckily, I really liked the name so it wasn't a problem at all. I have always wondered what would have happened if I didn't like the name.

Jay was still working at the ASB when Jason was born. When Jason was about a month old, Jay asked me to bring him to his office so we could, once again, make the rounds to all of his friends' offices, this time to introduce our baby to them. We had a Chrysler Lebaron convertible that we soon realized was not the ideal family car. When the top was down, the wind would blow in Jason's face in the back seat, and he would cry. Also, it wasn't easy to get a baby in and out of a backward-facing car seat in a two-door car. Parenthood was quickly changing our lifestyle, and we loved every minute of it.

I left the position in admissions with BYU in 1990. It had been a wonderful stage of my life. Of all the things I took from my time at BYU, I think learning to listen was the most gratifying skill I acquired. Listening and really understanding what someone was saying helped me to respond better as a person, as a husband, and eventually as a father.

I look back at those years and remember how I felt a little strange (especially at first) to go from being a producer/performer to a counselor/representative. I worked in a position which normally required a minimum of a master's degree, and I hadn't even received my bachelor's degree at the time.

In 1990, I decided to go to school full-time so I could move closer to getting my degree. Kandilyn was pregnant with Eric at the time. We'd moved from our house in Provo and into a condo I purchased from my sister. I had an intern class I needed to complete, which was a requirement within my major of "Speech Communications." Since the internship was with Morris Travel in Salt Lake City (60 miles away from Provo), I thought it would make sense to make another move. Kandi agreed, and we looked for a house in Sandy, Utah.

I also had it in my mind that since I traveled all my life, working at a travel agency would be an easy thing to do. It didn't take long for me to experience a reality wake-up call, because working for Morris Incentive Travel was one of the toughest things I have ever tried.

I not only had an internship with them, but eventually worked for them for about a year. I mainly focused on putting together incentive trips for organizations. The training I had at BYU really came in handy when working with clients and internal office support. I hadn't realized how much work was required to be effective at marketing and sales. My positions at BYU had prepared me somewhat for recruiting, office work and counseling; but, the marketing aspect was a whole new world for me. Even the marketing we use in show business couldn't compare to the stress that was put on us at Morris Travel. Ever since this experience, I have a great respect for people in this line of work, especially for two people there named Bill Jensen and Leann Foutz.

I'm grateful for the experience at Morris Travel and feel I really learned a lot. It opened my mind to others more and how people deal with the pressures, worries, and concerns of life. It also taught me that even though my entertainment career had taken me to countless places, and I met people from all walks of life, there was still a very big world out there.

I was beginning to drift when it came to what I needed to do to provide for my little family. My reserves were running low, so I looked at the possibility of working for my friend at Red Lion Hotels in a management position. However, this idea just really didn't seem right to Kandi or me.

While I was taking a couple of classes at Salt Lake Community College, the admissions director, Larry Landward (who had become a good friend of mine while at BYU) offered me a job. I was about to say yes to that when I received a phone call from my brother Jimmy that was definitely going to change my career path—and our life as we knew it.

I had gone through a period wondering if the "grass was

greener" on the other side; but I obviously never lost that identity of being an Osmond Brother. It just came naturally.

For a long while, I believed the entertaining stage of my life was gone and that my days of performing with my brothers were over. My hope though, was to find a way to work with them again, without some of the travel and craziness that goes along with performing.

Act 8

~1991–2000~

BRANSON BOUND

ERIC CLINTON OSMOND

It was 1990, and we were in the process of moving from Provo to Sandy, Utah. I had just finished my experience working at BYU, and we were on to another chapter. Kandi was pregnant with Eric, and it was a scary time for us.

I'll never forget going to the doctor to see how our little baby was doing when Kandi was expecting Eric. During one visit, the doctor said our baby was no longer there. With tears in our eyes, we set the appointment for Kandi to have a D&C. As the time came closer to that appointment, I felt, as did Kandi and her doctor, that we should have an ultrasound to check one more time to see if there was any sign of life. I am so thankful to this day, because the doctor said to us, "You are not going to believe what is showing up!" There was a little baby heartbeat appearing on the screen. Eric Clinton was hanging on! Thank goodness we followed our promptings. His nickname, even to this day, is "Bright Spot" —that priceless blip on the monitor screen. Kandi explains what life was like during this period.

Jason was the only child for two years and four months. When we found out we were expecting Eric, we were living at the Georgetown Condominiums in

Provo, Utah, and finishing the construction of our new home in Sandy. Once again, Jay was ecstatic when I told him we were expecting. Unfortunately, I started repeatedly hemorrhaging very early in the pregnancy, and we were terrified we would lose our baby. I ended up being on bed rest for four months. We were even mistakenly told that we had lost Eric twice. It was a difficult time for us but worth every minute to get our Eric here.

I decided on Eric's name, having selected it as I looked through a book of baby names. I thought it was only fair that I got to pick our second child's name. We always knew we would use Clinton, my father's name, as Eric's middle name, since Jason's middle name was George (for Jay's father). We liked several names, but Eric became our definite choice after seeing Disney's *The Little Mermaid.* We still call Eric, "Prince Eric."

On January 2, 1991, Eric was born in Murray, Utah at Cottonwood Women's Center. Once again Jay was with me for the birth. The Women's Center was a very nice place to have a baby. The birthing rooms were set up to look like beautiful hotel suites instead of sterile hospital rooms. There was even a big Jacuzzi tub in the bathroom that was attached to the room. Jay was feeling nervous, so the nurse suggested he get in the tub to relax for a while. While Jay was in the Jacuzzi, I called my parents to tell them the baby was coming. I had to laugh when they asked how Jay was holding up. I told them where he was and they seemed rather shocked. Times certainly had changed since they had their children and my dad was confined to a waiting room.

While I was expecting Eric, Jay was "retired." He was no longer working and had become "Mr. Mom" because I was bedridden with my pregnancy. He thought he could retire at age 36 and enjoy it. He was mistaken. The timing of this attempt at retirement was extremely fortunate since I needed his help at home so desperately, but it just didn't feel right. Jay knew he needed to work, if only for his own sanity. He said the day he realized there was something wrong with him being retired at 36 years old happened while Jason was outside playing with the neighborhood children. Jay was standing with a group of moms, and they were talking about Tupperware. Yes, that was the moment Jay realized he was out of place. Needless to say, once I was on my feet his "retirement" ended.

We were four years into our marriage, living in Sandy, Utah, and Eric was just a year old when a problem that strikes so many couples hit my little family. After four years of marriage, Kandi and I found we were really at odds with each other. The stresses of life were beginning to take their toll. Kandilyn was having a hard time dealing with the obsessive/compulsive side of me, and I was dealing with her anxiety and depression. Everything began to snowball. All the little things were starting to make our marriage fall apart. I got an apartment in Salt Lake City, and we ended up being separated for four months. I am so glad we got into marriage counseling, because our wonderful counselor Dr. Scoresby helped us both to reach a real turning point in our lives. Working things out and getting back together was one of the best things we've ever done. Our marriage has become nothing but stronger ever since.

BACK IN SHOWBIZ . . . WITH NEW TERMS

In 1992, my family and I were living in Sandy, Utah, and I was getting close to making a decision to either work at Salt Lake Community College or take a marketing position that was offered to me with Red Lion Hotels. Then, one particular day, I answered the phone, and it was my brother Jimmy. He wanted to tell me about his experience in a place called Branson, Missouri. As he excitedly talked about buying a theater there and getting the brothers together again to perform at it, something clicked inside of me like turning on a light. I knew this idea of Jimmy's was the right thing to do.

As we spoke, we discussed the new terms, or rather, the conditions under which I would go back into show business. Jimmy would be in charge, and things would be run in much more of a business-type way than some of our past ventures in entertainment.

I was excited about the prospect of getting back into entertaining with the ability to go home to my family at the end of each day. Just as pieces of a puzzle start to fit together, Jimmy's idea progressed, and I knew the move was a good one.

I felt like I was back in my element but with more wisdom, having worked in different fields other than show business. I feel that working at BYU and Morris Incentive Travel brought a whole new perspective and value to working in show business. It was all worth it, and those experiences could be used for future situations in my life.

Branson

I loved the idea that we would be performing in one place and that the lifestyle would be conducive to raising our boys. By not having to travel, I felt we could live the normal life we were accustomed to, and our boys would have a normal upbringing while they got a feel for my job as an entertainer. I definitely felt more comfortable in my work, being back in my element.

I hoped that life would not be as crazy and chaotic as it had been in the past when my brothers and I performed together. I took the good I learned from those six years away from entertainment and applied what I learned to a business that is hard to control. This worked, and I am so glad we made the decision to go to Branson. Kandi states:

> Jay continued to work at BYU after we were married. He didn't return to show business until 1992. I never knew him as an entertainer until then.
>
> When he started working in Branson, I was really excited to see him on stage. I had seen him play the drums and sing one or two songs with his brothers but never saw him perform a whole show. I remember just being blown away when I first saw him perform in Branson.

The idea of entertaining in Branson appealed to me, because I believed it not only was a great opportunity, but one that would allow us to keep our children grounded and not get caught up in the craziness of show business. This was a way of doing what I was trained to do but still have a normal (so to speak) lifestyle and a good atmosphere for my little family.

A Wild Ride to Cincinnati

We were scheduled to take a break from our grueling schedule in Branson and perform a show with The Platters for a bus tour convention that was being held in Cincinnati, Ohio. We obviously had to be there in time for the convention, but the pilot warned us that we might not be able to make the scheduled flight because the weather conditions we'd be flying into were bad. We decided to take the flight anyway, taking our chances as the plan was to fly on the outskirts of the storms. We were divided into two groups of people on two small jets. The plane I was on managed to fly on the outer edge of the bad weather, but it was quite a nightmare of a storm and came up fast. Wayne was on the other plane, along with The Platters and Jay Brandon from our band. Wayne said the three heaviest guys of the group were sitting at the back of the plane, and he was seated up near the cockpit. Things became very scary as the plane Wayne was in did a 360 degree roll while he watched it on the instrument panel. Wayne suddenly felt ice all around him and for a moment thought the plane had opened up. He thought it was the elements outside but soon realized the icy feeling was ice from an ice chest. All three of the men toward the back of the plane were floating in the air and hit the ceiling because they were in a down draft and didn't have their seat belts on. One of the ladies from The Platters panicked—understandably—thinking she was going to die; Wayne said there was a lot of screaming. It is interesting what happens to people when they think they are going to meet the end. In my plane it was a little less horrific; thanks to being more on the outskirts of the storm, we just experienced extreme turbulence. Fortunately, we got through it and made it to our scheduled performance. It reminded me of the time when I was ten years old and made that flight for a performance with Andy Williams. It was another "show must go on" test of our ability to recover quickly and perform as scheduled.

There were so many happy times in Branson that it was almost too good to be true. Kandilyn's family was in Utah, so she missed them quite a bit; but other than that, we loved our life. We did everything together. The hardest part was after the first show. Each day I would go home, relax, and play with our boys; and then when it came time to go back for the second show, I would have an energy drop. Fortunately, once I got on stage I was right back in the groove.

Living and working in Branson was a very unique situation for our family, and the timing was great. My kids, being young, needed me around a lot. It really just all worked out perfectly for that time in our lives.

When I contemplated going back to performing, I sometimes wondered what it would be like to have fans again. I quickly found it felt very comfortable. My whole life has been based on family and fans. My mother always thought of fans as friends, and this is my perception, as well.

I love thinking back on this time in our lives. A typical day in Branson would involve playtime in between the boys' school day and my performances at the theater. If I wasn't at the theater, I was home with Kandi and the kids. On Sundays, it was church, home teaching, and missionary work. I was the ward missionary leader for eight of the nine years we lived in Branson, which meant I didn't see my family much on Sundays after church. However, having all of that priceless time spent at home during the week more than made up for any time I had to spend away. I always counted my blessings that I was never very far away from them.

I think one of my fondest memories from those years involved my father and mother. In between shows, I would often walk over to see my parents, who had a house within walking distance of the theater. Every time I went there, either with my kids or by myself, my parents would always fix me something to eat. Usually, it was an onion and tomato sandwich (seriously!). I'd have to use mouthwash a few times before the second shows, but it was so worth it. I have many memories of the fun talks and walks with my parents in Branson, and I'll treasure that time forever.

Torn Ligaments and a Bruised Ego

During the late 1970s, I used to play church softball a lot. There would be girls hanging around and watching, which is just enough incentive to get the old ego into overdrive. One time, I didn't warm up my arm because I thought I was still in shape from playing football. A guy, who the girls obviously thought was pretty cool, showed up to play. He was stealing my thunder, which really bugged me, so I thought I'd show him what it was to be cool! I went to center field, and he hit one over my head, yelling, "Osmond, show your stuff!" I ran like mad to get to the ball as he headed around the bases and was making his way towards third base. Feeling very determined, I bulleted the ball from way out in center field and got it home just as he was heading in. It was amazing! But my throw resulted in more than making it to home base in the nick of time; it also caused me to tear some of the ligaments in my shoulder. My arm was never the same after that. Bottom line: Always warm up, and watch that ego!

In the 1980s we produced various shows, and I was putting together a show for the U.S. Ski Team. Unfortunately, all of the guests I had lined up for the show fell through with the exception of two. The ski team was really appreciative of my efforts, though, and made me an honorary member of the U.S. Ski Team (though I'm by no means a great skier). Years later, I thought it would be fun to go skiing with my son Eric at the Sundance Resort. Eric told some of his friends that I once worked with the U.S. Ski Team and they seemed really impressed. Eric asked me if I remembered any of the techniques that I learned from working with those great Olympic athletes. I said, "I think so." We were at the top of a hill, and as I headed down the hill in pursuit of Eric, I flew out of control, rolled, and a ski went flying. I rolled again and again, and finally stopped—rather abruptly. By showing off, I once again injured some of the ligaments in my shoulder. I learned we're never so good that we don't need to warm up; being given honorary titles doesn't make us experts; and egos really do get bruised.

The 1990s were full of wonderful memories. Kandilyn and I loved having our little family, and we were living a wonderful life in Branson with me performing at The Osmond Family Theater and able to go home at the end of each day. I was able to take the boys with me to work if I wanted, and they even joined me on stage from time to time. However, I never once pushed show business on them. I let them experience it with a little exposure on stage in Branson but decided I would never encourage or downplay the entertainment business. I wanted them to come to their own decision about it.

A Near Miss with George W. Bush

Before he was President of the United States and while he was the Governor of Texas, we made an appearance with George W. Bush. There was a big home improvement show being held there, and Alan, Wayne, Merrill, Jimmy, and I were invited to perform. Mr. Bush was also making an appearance, but he didn't come to rehearsal; because of that, he didn't know there were going to be indoor fireworks. He came and stood next to me as we sang "God Bless America," and when the fireworks went off, Mr. Bush was caught by surprise (that is an understatement). He grabbed me, and we hit the ground along with one of the singers from the show. When he realized the sudden noises were fireworks and not gun shots, we stood back up and he brushed himself off as the song continued. I knew he had to be embarrassed beyond words, but he carried on barely missing a beat. Governor Bush later explained he was trained to drop whenever there is a sudden loud noise like that. The situation is pretty comical to me now.

MARCUS JAY OSMOND

Marcus's entry into this world came on January 8,1996, while we were living in Branson, Missouri. Marcus was a real kicker and stormed into this world—quite literally. On the day of his arrival, I asked our good friends the Haynies (at 3:00 A.M.) to watch Jason and Eric so Kandilyn and I could get to the hospital for the birth of our third child. We were anxiously trying to get to the hospital, but it was slow going because of terrible, icy roads. We made it halfway to Springfield and knew we had to resort to calling for an ambulance. Marc was letting us know he was coming very soon! The ambulance finally arrived, and it was all so exciting that I took pictures of the whole thing (Kandi was not amused). They took Kandi, and I followed in our car. I was numb, not knowing what was going on in that ambulance. Parading in my mind were horrible thoughts; but at the same time I hoped for the best and prayed in my heart that all would be well. Marc certainly made sure that his grand entrance into this world was a big one. Thankfully, he managed to hold on until we got to the hospital. We knew this was our last baby, and what a relief it was to hear that deep, low cry of his come out and the doctor saying everything was okay. Kandi remembers the time well:

We had trouble getting our precious Marcus here. We knew we wanted a third child, but I had suffered a miscarriage in January of 1990. So, we were both excited and relieved when we found out later that year we were expecting again.

Marc was born at St Joseph's Hospital in Springfield, Missouri, during an ice storm. There was a lot of drama with this delivery—my water breaking in the middle of the night, having to get an ambulance because of the weather, and then my doctor breaking his foot right after delivering Marcus. It was an unbelievable series of events.

The moment Marcus was born Jay and I were struck by how deep his little cry was. He was also our biggest baby. We knew he was going to be a big, tough guy.

We enjoyed saying, "My Three Sons," like the old television show that starred Fred MacMurray. I came up with Marc's name; and Jay agreed. We were going to name him Marcus Ian for months, until one day at dinner a few weeks before he was born. Jason (who was seven at the time) said, "Why are you going to name him Ian? Why don't you give him a special middle name like Eric and I have? Why don't you name him Marcus Jay, after Dad?" We loved the idea!

It felt quite natural for us to have boys. I have three younger brothers, and Jay has seven brothers (and a lot of nephews). Jay always said he was living his long lost childhood through our boys. Many times it felt like I was raising four boys instead of three. They loved anything physical, messy, and adventurous. I've cleaned up a lot of messes over the years.

There are five years and six days between Marcus and Eric. This is not how we planned it, but we were just thrilled to get our Marcus here. After he was born,

Jay and I both immediately felt that our family was complete.

Kandilyn and I made it a point to be sure that our kids had a happy childhood. If you ask any of my boys to this day, they will each tell you that Branson was the perfect childhood. In fact, it was apparently too good. When we moved back to Utah after nine years of living in Branson, the kids were almost traumatized because life changed so drastically. Life in Utah was good but difficult, because my brothers and I started performing road dates again. The family togetherness and dynamics changed greatly. As Kandi explains:

> When Marcus was born, Jay was working at the Osmond Family Theater in Branson, Missouri. Our two older boys and I had been appearing in the Christmas shows (and occasionally in the summer shows) for four years. After Marcus came, we just kept right on doing the shows as a family.
>
> Show business is not a business I would have ever wanted my children involved with in a million years, but the theater was like being part of a big family, so it didn't concern me. As long as the kids were enjoying it, we did it.
>
> We've always felt that we would support our children in any career they chose, including show business, but we never wanted to specifically push them in that direction. We both wanted our boys to have a normal childhood; and, despite the occasional comment or extra attention they receive from classmates and teachers, they have.

A Bad Example and Road Rage

I used to think it was good to teach my children about driving when my kids were in the car with me. If I saw someone driving poorly, or someone riding a bicycle in traffic, I would shout things like: "That turkey needs to get off the road!" or "Get out of traffic!"

My thinking was that I was teaching my kids what was safe and what wasn't.

One day my son Eric said he didn't like to be in the car with me, explaining that I yelled at people when I was inside the car. I had no idea that rather than teaching with example, I was upsetting Eric. I sat the boys down and asked if they all felt that way, and they said I was scary to drive with. Feeling bad about the example I was setting for them, I went to see my friend, who is a counselor. I asked how to teach kids to be safe besides making comments about poor drivers, etc. When I told him how the boys felt about being in the car with me, he said I had road rage. I was shocked.

He explained that fear and anger are one chemical apart from each other in the brain and proceeded to tell me a story that has stuck with me ever since. He knew someone who became very angry while driving. A driver cut him off and was driving erratically. This made him so mad—he wanted to pull him off the road and give him a piece of his mind. His anger persisted as he watched the driver, then he snapped. He decided to follow the "crazy driver." The driver pulled off the road (as he followed him) and then down the street and into the emergency entrance of a hospital. He then saw the driver pull a little boy out of the car and run into the emergency room with him. That angry man quickly realized the error of his ways.

We never truly know what someone else is experiencing, which is why it is so important not to pass judgment. Hearing this story changed me. I told the boys I would no longer yell at drivers or kids along the road if it appeared they weren't doing the right thing. To this day, if someone pulls in front of me, I always think, "I hope everything is okay."

Perception can be a funny thing. We all see things a little differently. For instance, when Marcus was little he told us he wanted to take a lunchbox to school like his friends. I quickly remembered one of the old Osmond lunchboxes was in my storage room. I ran and got it for him; and when I presented what I thought was a cool treasure for my son to carry to school with him, Marcus's response was, "Dad, I wouldn't be caught dead with this!"

SHOULD WE STAY OR SHOULD WE GO?

We had the perfect balance of an entertainment career and family life, so I've often been asked what prompted the decision in 2000 to leave Branson and move back to Utah. My little family was doing great in Branson. Our kids were happy; and though Kandilyn felt a little homesick for her family and for Utah, she did well. I loved it there. I finally found a place where I could do for a living what was comfortable for me and have a structured family lifestyle, as well.

Alan had to leave the group when his multiple sclerosis made it too difficult for him to keep up with our busy performance schedule. Alan's boys, who also spent some time performing at our theater, eventually all left for missions and afterwards moved back to Utah. Wayne and Merrill's families also moved back to Utah. Father and Mother moved to Ephraim, Utah, so they could be closer to my brother Tom, as well as to a lot of the grandchildren. Virl and his wife, Chris, were in Branson quite a bit helping us with the shows and doing public relations work. Being in Branson caused Wayne and Merrill to have to spend too much time away from their families. Jimmy and I both had our families with us, but Wayne and Merrill increasingly became dissatisfied with performing in Branson. The rather grueling schedule of two shows a day, six days a week, year after year had taken a toll on all of us. We eventually decided it was time we started to wind Branson down and do more road dates. There was still a big market out there for us than just Branson; and by performing on the road, Wayne and Merrill could go home more often to see their families. Since Kandilyn's parents were living in Utah, it made sense for us to move back there. With me being on the road most of the year, she could at least be near her family.

Initially, our boys didn't handle the move from Missouri to Utah well; in fact, I was really worried about them. I tried to explain to them that I would be going back to performing "on the road" and that our life as we knew it was going to change in a new and exciting way. Unfortunately, life actually got tougher for the boys, for Kandilyn, and for me.

We had all been used to spending so much time together, and now I was working on the road, sometimes for months at a time. This was difficult for Kandilyn. Not only did we miss each other terribly, but she was a bit overwhelmed with three young boys on her own. Life was going the way Wayne and Merrill wanted, while things became more challenging for my little family and for Jimmy's. But for some reason, I knew as tough as it was for us, it was the right thing to do in the long run.

The day finally came when we left the familiar routine at the Osmond Family Theater, and it was time to say goodbye to that stage of my life. I was really torn. It was a bittersweet kind of feeling. There were so many happy memories and yet some hard ones, too.

For a while, my family was back in Utah, and I was finishing up the fall and Christmas seasons in Branson without them. We'd sold the house, and our two cats were living with me in a condo I owned in town. I don't think I've ever experienced a harder time in my life.

My wife and kids were adjusting to living in Provo, Utah without me for several months while I was wrapping up things in

Branson. Kandilyn was being "super mom" by getting the kids into all kinds of activities, unpacking, etc.

I think this is where I really became close to our wonderful pets. It broke my heart to have to find a new owner for Zeek. Kandilyn was allergic to that cat, and we knew Zeek wouldn't be able to make the trip to Utah like Isaac could, so we had to make a hard decision. We found a wonderful couple from Arkansas who opened up their home to Zeek. I made two trips to Arkansas just to be sure they were taking good care of her.

It felt like losing a loved one. I was angry, sad, depressed, and moody just thinking about—and missing—Zeek. This might have been the first time when I really understood the important role pets play in our lives. I had pets in the past, as I've mentioned, but these cats grew up with our boys. They were important to our whole family. I later shared what I have gained from having pets in my life with my friends Terri and Jeff Shoemaker. Terri explains:

> I'd been assisting Jay for about a year, and he decided he wanted to bring a cat into my life. He'd introduced me to their kitty, Isaac. I was never a "cat person," so I think my uneasiness showed. Jay put Isaac into my arms, and the cat flew out of my grasp. Jay didn't give up, though. My husband, Jeff, and I were on one of the brothers' road dates, and Jay took Jeff aside. My birthday was coming, and I later learned that Jay and Jeff concocted a plan for Jay and his family to give me a kitten for my birthday. This was quite a risky thing for Jay to do, but he knew at least Jeff would gladly welcome the pet. I was presented with a kitten we named "Jo Jo" (using Jay's initials, with the Osmond hit "Yo-Yo" in mind). Jo Jo grabbed a piece of my heart so fast, it made my head spin. In fact, Jeff and I added to our family three months later by adopting a kitten we named "Elvis Wesley." A few years later, a third kitten ("Allie Cat," a stray) found her way into our family. Jay knew he had enriched our lives with his birthday gift and opened

up a whole new side of me I didn't know existed. Our kitties know their "Uncle Jay," and he's even spoiled them with fun kitty gifts from time to time. I'll always be grateful (as will Jeff) that Jay persisted in getting me that cat. He gave us a simple gift that will be a part of our lives, in one way or another, forever.

It has been said that a pet can have a healing effect on a person and can even make him or her live longer. I sincerely feel there is something to that school of thought.

Act 9

~2001—2009~

BACK ON THE ROAD AGAIN

HITTING THE ROAD

The Branson routine became a thing of the past, and performing on the road was a part of my life once again. At first, it didn't bother me to be back on the road, though it was an adjustment after being in a set routine for so many years. After a while, the road really affects me. It is the waiting in airports, the hassle of working out the time schedules, and all of the other business that goes with traveling that really drains me. Travel is definitely not the glamorous part of show business. I think I have "terminal" illness—I'm allergic to airports.

Wayne, Merrill, and I were no longer going to be performing regularly with Jimmy once we hit the road. Jimmy's other business activities didn't permit him to be with us a lot, so Wayne, Merrill, and I became a group of three. It was very hard for me, because it meant that Jimmy wouldn't be performing with us on a regular basis. He was the reason I came back to show business in the first place, so obviously this was a very hard decision for me.

The first part of this decade had a lot of milestones, drama, sadness, loss, achievement, and once-in-a-lifetime moments. ABC-TV aired a movie about our family in February of 2001 called, *Inside the Osmonds.* Jimmy was an executive producer of the movie, along with Robert M. Sertner, Frank von Zerneck, Merv Griffin, Mark Sennet, and Matt Dorff. Having Jimmy so involved made the whole idea of this movie more comfortable for me. I recall reading through the script, laughing hysterically at some of our antics during the 1970s. There were other scenes that were hard for me to read through—reminding me of the many highs and lows we've experienced as a family. It was so interesting when we got to meet the actors who played our characters. We each spent a little time with the actor portraying us so that they could get an accurate feel for who we really were—rather than just reading from a script.

It was great when Father, Mother, Virl, Tom, Alan, Wayne, Merrill, Donny, Marie, Jimmy, and I all went to Winnipeg, Manitoba, Canada in December 2000 to film the ending of the movie. There was a scene at the end where the actors faded out and turned into us—all of the "real" Osmonds. It was a great effect to end the movie, and kind of a surreal feeling. I think the movie came off positively, and it was an honor to have a movie made about our family at that point in our lives.

In the fall of 2002, in addition to performing spot dates around the country, Wayne, Merrill, and I had the opportunity to go back to Branson, Missouri. We performed a morning show for a season at the Country Tonite Theater. Jimmy had projects in England; Donny and Marie were each performing in theater; Virl was working on his degree; Alan was pioneering his websites; Father and Mother were being cute grandparents; and Tommy was winning the hearts of everyone in Ephraim, Utah as a postal carrier.

The following season in 2003 was like coming full circle when we performed at Andy Williams' Moon River Theater in Branson. The three of us are not "morning people," so these two seasons of performing morning shows were tough.

We had a really cool event come along that year when U.K.'s ITV came to us with the proposal to film a documentary for primetime television called, *Being the Osmonds*. The documentary brought all six performing Osmond Brothers (Alan, Wayne,

Merrill, Donny, Jimmy, and myself) together onstage at Andy Williams' Moon River Theater. It really was a special reunion and was filmed live on May 5, 2003.

August 7, 2003 brought another huge honor to our family in Los Angeles, California. We received a star on Hollywood's Walk of Fame. (Sadly, Mother was not able to be there with us because of the stroke she had suffered, and Virl stayed in Utah to tend to her.) This truly was a memorable day for my family and for our fans.

It was really shaping up to be an amazing decade for us as a family. Later that year, we were honored to perform for Her Majesty Queen Elizabeth II and His Royal Highness The Duke of Edinburgh at the 75th Royal Variety Performance held in Edinburgh on November 24, 2003. What an experience; we were so honored when we received two standing ovations. I was especially proud to be able to have my oldest son Jason experience this with me.

While at this performance, I remember having to go the restroom, which was located just outside our dressing rooms. I saw there was a guard standing outside the restroom and asked if there was someone in it. The guard replied, "Me lady is in the loo." I was quite surprised to learn that the Queen was right there in the restroom! I went back to the dressing room and told Jason, and just then we heard the toilet flush. The timing of telling Jason the Queen was in the restroom couldn't have been better had it been planned. Jason started laughing and said, "Dad, do you know what a royal flush is in a game of cards?" I said "yes," and he said, "Well, now you've heard one!"

Act 9, Scene 2

OPENING A NEW DOOR

The decade started off with some amazing experiences, but life always brings lows along with the highs. In 2004, after we toured for a while, Wayne and Merrill made the decision to change the act and direction of the brothers. I wasn't comfortable with this direction, and Kandi and I felt it was time for me to make a clean break (like I did back in 1985). I decided to attempt to learn the business of real estate.

Making this decision was a tough thing for me. I was concerned about finances and felt a lot of pressure to be a good realtor quickly. I was constantly working, and the cell phone never stopped ringing. There were some good moments, but overall it was very difficult for me. I had wonderful trainers, Fay Jones and Jeff Mendenhall, and I was really grateful to have them to work with.

I liked the idea that I could be out and about a lot. I liked the fact that it was very challenging, both mentally and socially. I had to really use the left side of my brain a lot and think through things very carefully. This was something I needed to work on.

Real estate also taught me to pay attention to detail. This is something I've tried to remember as I deal with other aspects of life.

The reason I felt comfortable going into real estate was that my father started the company I was working for, so I didn't feel completely estranged by the fact that I was working at something other than entertaining. Being an Osmond working at Osmond Real Estate, my identity was tied in. With Jimmy being the owner of Osmond Real Estate, this was another reason for me to be comfortable with the change.

My father was really pleased with me for trying my hand at this. In fact, a local paper did an article with a big picture of my father and me (unfortunately, Jimmy was in England at the time). It was a cool father/son moment with a business setting.

Initially, working at Osmond Real Estate felt a little like being a fish out of water; but it was nothing like the feeling I had when I worked at BYU. At BYU, I definitely felt like a porcupine in a balloon factory. At Osmond Real Estate, I felt more accepted and free to make mistakes. I even had a drawer in my desk at the office which was labeled "gaffes," or in other words, "blunders." I laughed at all the goof-ups I made, instead of worrying about them like I did at BYU.

I felt an identity shift in my life once again. I really think, though, it was good for me to expand and do more things on my own. I didn't realize how strong my group identity was until I had these experiences both at BYU and Osmond Real Estate.

One of the thrills of my life was around 2002–03, when I was asked to be an adjunct professor at UVSC (now UVU). As part of working toward my degree, I was invited to teach with the Dean of the College of Engineering and Technology, Tom McFarland. Tom and I became friends as we taught "Marketing and the Media." He taught the technical side of the class, and I handled the creative side. We had about 25 students in the class. I learned that I could actually teach a class at a college level, and it was a great step forward for me.

Life moved along working as a real estate agent; then one day, my brother Donny played his video of a performance in Wales for me. The video showed Donny performing a new version of

"Crazy Horses" that he was excited for me to see. As I watched him perform the song, one of my kids said, "You used to do that song, didn't you, Dad?" I felt a little cringe inside and said, "I've got to go back!" I missed show business and realized I'd been fighting those familiar feelings of being on stage with my brothers and seeing the faces of the people in the audience.

Act 9, Scene 3

QUANDARY

At the beginning of 2005, I was a little mixed up. I wasn't sure what I really wanted to do. Real estate was crazy, and I became too obsessed with it. I liked teaching but felt I didn't have the patience and time necessary to devote to correcting and grading papers. Show business was comfortable for me. With these things in mind, and knowing how travel affects me, I made the decision to just do "spot dates," such as cruises, Branson Christmas shows, and occasional road dates—and see what happened after that.

In addition to all of the feelings I was having about what I wanted (and needed) to do, there was always the desire to get my degree. Going back to performing would obviously again slow down the progress of working toward that goal, but my plan was to keep working on it.

We performed in Branson again, but it really never was the same for me. My family visited on several occasions; but as I learned long ago at USU, you can't go back and try to relive old memories. You instead end up making new ones.

After leaving the routine of performing in Branson, and instead working at various theaters year after year, things definitely changed. The one gig that *really* changed things in my mind forever came along. It was when Wayne, Jimmy, and I played Blackpool, Lancashire, England with Billy Pearce. This show was one of the funniest I have ever seen. It was like being in a play, while still being an Osmond. The structure of it was great, too. It was like going to work every day (except Sunday) and having a normal life. It really felt good to perform with my brothers in this capacity. It was structured like a play: we weren't just Osmonds, we were part of a production, and I liked that aspect of it. It was the ultimate experience for me and a highlight of my career. Performing in Sweden back in the 1960s is the only highlight that could top it.

A Wrong Turn in Wales

When I was performing with my brothers Wayne and Jimmy in Blackpool, Kandi and the boys came out for a visit. The shows came to a close in Blackpool, and my family and I set out to return home to Utah. Kandi, Jason, Eric, Marcus, and I were driving our rental car to the airport, unaware that the airport was in the middle of an alert because of a bomb threat. I made a wrong turn and was driving down the wrong side of the road. All of a sudden, I saw lights from police cars coming at me. They stopped us by blocking the car, and like an idiot I got out of the vehicle. They immediately pulled out their guns—even machine guns! Kandi was screaming for me to get back into the car. Eric started screaming, "We're going to die; they're going to shoot Dad!" Marcus was crying. And Jason was pretty much in shock. The police came up to the car holding their guns on me, pushed me against the car, put my hands behind my back, and began to interrogate me. I said I was really sorry and I wasn't a criminal. They asked why I was driving on the wrong side of the road, and I tried to calm myself so I didn't appear to be an out-of-control person scared out of my mind (all while my wife and kids were panicking in the car). Finally they heard what I was trying to say, realized I was an Osmond, and was as goofy as I was saying—I had just made a mistake. I discovered the road I turned onto was not open to the public; and since the airport was under alert, we obviously caused serious concern to security. Moral of the story: never leave home without your GPS.

Leaving Real Estate

It didn't take too long to realize that I had no problem leaving real estate behind. I learned some great things and felt I really grew, but I was happy to get out of that rat race. There is something to be said for doing what you're comfortable with; and after stretching myself by working in another field, I felt much more enriched as a performer.

I really feel comfortable on stage when all is working well. When the sound is good out in the house and on stage, then it's comfortable. When the technical things don't go well, and things start to get chaotic, I get uptight. Also, when we are struggling with our voices or our energy levels are down, I start pushing too hard. Having worked outside of show business and experiencing other pressures and stress, I can clearly see that every job has its challenges.

I learned a lot about myself during this particular time. It almost felt like I'd gone full circle. In show business, you learn to try to meet the expectations of the public. Your image can die out quickly with the public if you are not careful; and if your self-image isn't strongly grounded, you can go down with it. I learned how important it is to not "personalize" business. If we can separate our personal selves from our professional selves—the "products" we are marketing—we will have the strength to make it through anything. I love how Jimmy uses the phrase, "Show business is the business of show." Doing other things besides performing on stage has really increased my appreciation for other occupations and, no matter what the vocation, how important it is to leave it all behind when you go home at the end of the day.

A Change of Heart

I'll never forget a particular time we were in Hawaii—I think it was sometime around 1978. Donny's success had soared, and a lot of people were treating him differently. He was having a very hard time finding a way to separate Donny the product from Donny the person. I think it all just came crashing down around him when a well-known newspaper writer negatively went after Donny and his music. He felt as though he was being ripped apart and just curled up with tears in his eyes. My heart went out to him, and I knew something had to change. We had quite a lengthy discussion about stepping outside of ourselves—and having a change of heart and mind. I believe what Donny needed to do is something anyone successful in the entertainment business needs to do . . . laugh! I repeated Mother's favorite line, "We are going to laugh about it someday, so why not laugh now?" However, at a very tender age, Donny wasn't able to see the humor. As I mentioned before, the "product" has to be separated from the person. After a few hours of heart-to-heart talking, Donny began to realize that one man's opinion of him didn't really matter. If ever some things are said negatively and actually have some validity, then we can take from that and learn. Constructive criticism is always good, but self love and self respect are so important. If we can truly see that we are all children of God and know that we are truly loved by Him, we can get through anything.

In the summer of 2005, Wayne, Merrill, Jimmy, and I joined Les McKeon's Bay City Rollers, David Cassidy, and David Essex for the *Once in a Lifetime Tour* in cities throughout the United Kingdom. It was really fun to see these guys in different situations. All of the performers were really cool. I thought David Cassidy was great. I thought David was Kandi's favorite performer, so I had the two of them meet, with less-than-stellar results! Kandi explains:

> When we were first married, I mentioned to Jay that the only poster of a pop star I ever had on my wall while growing up was Shaun Cassidy. It was a foldout from an album I had when I was about 11 or 12 years old and featured Shaun standing by a piano, dressed in white with a striped scarf. Jay has always remembered this story, and I occasionally tease him by saying he once had a rival for my heart in Shaun.

Jay has always been extremely kind and thoughtful. He will do anything in his power to try to make someone happy, even if he occasionally mixes up certain details. I'll never forget the time the kids and I joined Jay and his family in the U.K. for the last few days of their *Once in a Lifetime Tour.* Jay greeted me with a smile and said he had a big surprise for me. He said he talked with my teen idol, told him the story about how I was a big fan, and made special arrangements for me to meet him. You can imagine my embarrassment as I suddenly found myself in a quiet room, face to face with David, not Shaun, Cassidy. Later that year, I found a copy of the poster of Shaun and attached it to a wall in our house with a post-it note that said, "This was my teen idol."

This decade really was the beginning of a big rollercoaster ride of emotions for me. In February/March 2006, we went back to the U.K. for another tour. My brother Alan joined us towards the end of it, and a DVD, *Live at the Apollo Theater in London,* was filmed to document our reunion in the U.K.

Before my parents passed, I asked them what their thoughts were about passing on. They were both torn. They always taught us that you can create heaven on earth, and both of them did just that. My mother was such a stalwart in the Gospel. She really knew where she was headed after this life but wanted to stay longer to be there for us. As I sat by her bedside, I would remember the many times as a kid when I would run home and yell, "Mother!" Just hearing her voice say, "I'm right here" was all I needed. Now it was my turn to be there for her. She loved us, and she loved the wonderful people that followed the careers of her children.

With each loss, so many people made donations in our parents' names to the Children's Miracle Network. This was the perfect tribute to two wonderful people who had the vision to start this foundation to help children many years ago. Life goes on, and the losses sting a little bit less with each day. I find comfort in knowing that my parents touched so many lives and were such great examples of serving our Savior while on this earth.

Our entire family was scheduled to appear on *The Oprah Show* when Father passed, and we were left with the numbing decision of what we should do. Father always taught us the "show must go on," so we knew in our hearts he would want us to make that trip to Chicago as planned. With heavy hearts, we all piled into a private jet sent by Oprah—over 100 Osmonds. The event turned into more of a celebration of our father's life than a celebration of our entertainment careers. I think it was good for all of us to be together like that, and I know our parents were right there with us. Following *The Oprah Show,* we all trekked back to Utah for the funeral of our beloved father. It was another rollercoaster ride of emotions over those few days, and it was once again amazing to see the outpouring of love coming from people all over the world.

Act 9, Scene 4

50TH ANNIVERSARY

As we drew closer to the Osmond Brothers' 50th anniversary in entertainment, it became increasingly important to me that we did something special to celebrate with all of those who followed our careers. We started planning for our 50th anniversary celebration long before the kick-off in August 2007 at The Orleans in Las Vegas, Nevada. We were originally thinking about Disneyland and then considered Salt Lake City. As we continued tossing around ideas, my brothers and I started reminiscing about all the memorable times we had in Vegas with entertainers such as Elvis Presley, Frank Sinatra, and Andy Williams. We finally came to the agreement that Las Vegas would be the perfect place, since we had so much history there and it was a convenient location for our fans to come together.

I was really happy with how everything fell into place. It was a whirlwind and a lot of work, and it reminded me of the 1970s—it just didn't stop. Jimmy and I actually started work on the production about a year before the event. We spent countless hours gathering old photos, pulling together video, and working on the set-up and music. It was also quite a feat to find a time when all nine of us could come together. We had a lot of help hammering out all of the details to make this celebration happen, and I knew every minute of hard work was going to be well worth it.

I have to say, I became very reminiscent during this time. I never thought we would make it to a 50-year celebration together. I remember how amazed I was that we were still performing together when we reached our 25th anniversary. I also recall thinking at that time that our 25th anniversary would most likely be our last anniversary celebration. The pace we kept up for all those years was so hard; I just never expected we could keep at it that long. So, needless to say, when our 50th anniversary came, it really felt like an accomplishment in the entertainment business.

Having our wonderful fans come to celebrate with us was much like the feeling I had when so many came to celebrate as we received the Star on Hollywood's Walk of Fame in August of 2003. I couldn't believe how many people came from all over the world in support of these events. Both events felt like a family reunion, with the music and the memories. It was a celebration for all of us and for all of the friendships our fans have made with each other.

The memories that have stayed with me the most from our 50th anniversary celebration are the backstage interactions with my brothers and sister, and doing interviews together again. I remember Merrill saying, "If nothing else happens after this, we've had a wonderful run here on earth together."

We started out with a three-day celebration at The Orleans in Las Vegas, August 12–14, 2007. The shows were being taped for a PBS special that aired in March 2008. The day before our first show at The Orleans, my sister, Marie, got an infection in her eyes. The swelling made her almost unrecognizable, and she was wearing sunglasses most of the time because of it. We were concerned for Marie when she said the medicine prescribed for the problem wasn't helping, so we gave her a Priesthood blessing (something that is very sacred in our religion). We had television interviews scheduled for the next day followed by the show that night. An hour before the interviews, the swelling started to go down. It was an absolute miracle! Marie's eyes were back to normal. Then, after our first of three shows that weekend, Donny lost his voice. The doctor told Donny if he pushed it any harder, he could rupture his throat and possibly cause permanent damage. Poor Donny couldn't even talk and was feeling panicked. We gave him a blessing that night that he could sing without pain and not cause damage to his throat. The next night Donny performed perfectly without any problems. The doctor said he never saw anything like it—and we know it was from the blessing he received.

In May and June 2008, we continued the celebration by coming together on stage as a family one more time. All seven performing Osmonds were there: Alan, Wayne, Merrill, Donny, Marie, Jimmy, and me. I wished Virl and Tom could have joined us for this. We performed throughout the United Kingdom and then went on to Australia, Taiwan, the Philippines, Singapore, and Malaysia. Our 50th Anniversary DVD even hit the #1 spot on the BBC Radio 1 Chart. It was quite an amazing time for us at that point in our careers.

I'll never forget looking out over the sea of faces at Wembley Arena in London. It is hard to put this experience into words. I saw the smiles and felt so much love coming from our audience. However, this was more than an audience; these were wonderful people who have been on this journey with my family as we all grew up together. All of us had been through many challenges and trials and had somehow helped one another along the way. This was more than a concert; it was a celebration of life and loyalty. I tried to capture it like a snapshot in my mind, because I knew a camera couldn't do this picture justice.

During this world tour, we did a lot of press and made various appearances talking about our 50th anniversary. A fun highlight for me was when we saw Neil Diamond at *The Jonathan Ross Show* in the U.K. We had a good time talking with Neil, and I got a big kick out of him saying he wanted to be an Osmond. (Neil's drummer, Ronnie Tutt, was one of my drumming heroes.)

The whole year ended up being a celebration of 50 years of entertaining, and it was a very magical time in our lives. I felt our parents were right there with us—I think we all felt it. I also know they were very happy that Virl and Tom were a part of the celebration. In my mind, our older brothers, Virl and Tom, never received the credit they deserved. It was because of them that we got into show business (as I mentioned, we started performing to earn money to buy them hearing aids and to send them on their missions). Virl and Tom were also the first deaf missionaries for The Church of Jesus Christ of Latter-day Saints. I think about how hard it must have been for them to grow up during those sensitive years to be in the background due to their handicap. I think of them both as the real heroes in our family.

DVDs, CDs, a television special, and a photo book were among the items created to document the Osmond Brothers' 50th year in the entertainment industry. It really became quite a celebration. In fact, the only thing missing was a commemorative lunchbox.

Our performance in July 2008 with the Mormon Tabernacle Choir and Orchestra at Temple Square in Salt Lake City, Utah was the official closure to our 50th Anniversary Celebration. I think that performance was when I felt the most pressure. These were our neighbors. We ended in the place we began: Our first show was at the Wheeler Machinery Company in the Salt Lake area when I was not quite yet three years old.

That performance with the choir was the hardest part of our 50th celebration for me. The rehearsal was difficult, and we had a lot of technical problems (which is a pet peeve of mine and has always been hard for me). Being a Mormon family, it was especially important to me that we made a good impression at this particular performance. When one thing goes wrong, it can cause everything to have glitches. I feel it is a miracle how everything came off so well. This performance as a family was more than likely the final one for Alan (because of his condition with Multiple Sclerosis), and I wanted it to be a happy memory for him, although I knew how emotional and difficult it would be for him.

I will never forget that memorable moment when we turned

around and faced the choir, and they sang one of our mother's favorite hymns to us: "God Be with You Till We Meet Again." We knew our parents were right there with us, and there wasn't a dry eye among us. We never actually sang with the choir before as a family, and my mother said many times how she hoped one day we could do something with them. I know she loved and cherished this moment as much as we did, and I truly believe there wasn't a more fitting way to end our celebration of 50 years as a family in entertainment.

There is a part of me that is now wondering if we are going to make it to our 75th anniversary—it would be quite amazing and, I suppose, not completely out of the question.

In September 2009, we once again performed at The Osmond Theater in Branson, Missouri. We'd been away from that theater for about eight years, and I never really thought I'd be performing there with my brothers again. I walked into the theater and looked at all of those pictures hanging on the walls of celebrities we've worked with over the years. It is hard to believe how many wonderful people we've met and how many great opportunities we've had to work with and get to know them. It is fun to have personal stories about these people, and I thought about how after meeting and working with them, they seemed like just regular people and not celebrities. As I reflect upon all of the people we've met and worked with, and all of the wonderful fans we have, I feel very blessed.

NOW WHAT?

When our father was 65 years old, I asked him how he felt being at the retirement stage of his life. He replied, "It isn't retirement, it is refinement." Our father didn't believe people should ever retire—he didn't like the word. He felt what retiring means to most people is that it is a time to take it easy and enjoy life. But, my father enjoyed life at every stage, and retirement (or refinement) was his time to do other things—especially to serve the Lord. He and my mother went on their first mission in 1981. After their two missions as directors for visitor centers for the church in Hawaii and England, their focus was to be there for their children, grandchildren, and great-grandchildren. They have stayed in each one of our lives.

As far as the Osmond Brothers are concerned, we have no plans to retire. We take it year by year. It is a nice way to go at this stage of our lives.

I can look at my brothers and know exactly what is on their minds—we know each other so well. We have little cues such as looks, hand signals, and sign language (which we've learned from Virl and Tom). I sometimes think I know my brothers better than

I know myself. We've been raised so close, it will be hard to say goodbye to our careers together when the time comes.

The hardest part is the pressure we put on ourselves to be good at our performance, so my goal is to have more fun on stage at this point in my life. The career milestones have been reached, and I hope things can now be more relaxed. I have learned the show must go on, regardless of how I feel. Now I hope I can get on stage and let little mishaps be funny, rather than stressful.

We've been blessed to do what we enjoy on stage. Our music is our way of communicating to people and to each other that life can be fun and good. Music is a language that transcends through words. It is a language that everyone understands. There is a feeling that comes from this universal language, and it evokes many emotions from people. Songs bring back different memories in our lives. Music is almost like a sense in and of itself—like a sixth sense. Even my deaf brothers can "feel" music. I've read many letters over the years from people who have said our music has helped them. To know that our music has touched people in this way is a tremendous reward. Music touches our souls, and to be a part of the music industry has been an honor. We've always felt our entertaining has been sort of a mission or ministry, and music has given us a bridge to link us to all those who have listened to us over the years.

My sons are learning that music can be an influence for good. I hope they will always use music to lift and inspire others, as I feel it is meant to be used. Recently, while performing, I found myself thinking about how interesting it is that we've set the stage for my three boys and my nephews and nieces. They could carry on and do what we've done. They would learn it takes a lot of dedication, but I believe any of them could do it if they really choose to. Because of the brand we started, they have the opportunity to move forward in a big way.

It is exciting to think of all that lies ahead for my sons, and someday, for their children. I also hope to one day be able to share with my grandchildren the musical journey I've had with my brothers and sister. I want to show them not only what we did, but also tell them how our lives were touched; and how our music touched the lives of those who listened to us. I'll tell them about our parents and the vision they had for us; and, though life's journey has bumps along the way, there can be a happy ending. I'll tell them how we were a family that worked together in a challenging industry, stayed together, loved one another, and served the Lord.

While on his mission from April 2008 to April 2010, our oldest son Jason emailed, "Can you believe I might be married a year from now?!" I thought how strange, yet amazing, that sounded to me. It also made me realize how there are so many things in my life yet to come.

Life is a Scout Camp

I was at Scout camp with Marcus during the summer of 2009. I did a lot of complaining, because I really dislike camping (especially when weather conditions bring temperatures to below zero at night). I was not prepared for this at all. I was amazed at how tough Marc is. Marcus finally said to me, "Dad, life is tough, but life is a Scout camp." He assured me I would make it through a week of bitter cold, tents, hiking in the snow, uncomfortable sleep, and whining kids (like me). Marcus reminded me that challenges are good for us, and we grow as a result of them. I felt humbled and grateful for the wisdom that was pouring out of him, and his message stuck with me. Life can be hard, but it's through these experiences that we learn to appreciate, learn compassion, and develop an understanding of who we are and our dependency upon the Lord Jesus Christ.

Stage Notes

QUOTES, STORIES, AND MEMORIES

INSPIRATIONAL STORIES

When I hear something that strikes a chord with me, I'm compelled to jot it down and save it. If I read something that hits home for a particular reason, I need to hang onto it. Cards, letters, favorite scriptures, newspaper articles, sayings, quotes, funny stories—I just can't help but throw these things into my "memory boxes" that Kandi has set up for me. My filing system is far from perfect, so along the way I've lost track of where some of the quotes I like so much have come from. Their meanings have definitely stuck with me—which, I suppose, is the most important part. I've got things saved from all stages of my life. These fragments of days past have become a part of who I am. Here are some of my favorites:

- My father once said, "Jay, if you learn from the things I did right, as well as from the things I did wrong, then you've learned."

- One time, when discussing why people have so many questions about our beliefs and sometimes make judgments about our church, my mother said, "If you're not up on something, you're usually down on it."

- There are many interpretations for what Ying/Yang means, but what it means to me is to learn to give and receive. If we can learn to do both gracefully, that is the ticket.

- This poem got me through a lot of tough times as a teenager:

Dare to Be a Mormon

Dare to be a Mormon
Dare to stand alone
Dare to have a purpose
And dare to make it known.

- I always remember the words my angel mother often used when things were tough: "This too shall pass!" Or, "We're going to laugh about this someday, so we might as well laugh about it now."

- When my oldest son Jason was leaving for his mission, I told him I wished I could have gone on a mission like him. His response to me was, "We are all down here on a mission, away from home. Our goal is to serve and help one another. None of us is home, yet!"

- In 2003 when we were in Scotland and about to go on stage for a performance for the Queen, I was feeling a little nervous and uptight. I said, "Let's just get this over with and go home." My son Jason stopped me and said, "Dad, this moment may never happen again. Do you realize how many people would love to be in your shoes? Just enjoy it." I've never forgotten my son's wise words.

- Our family was doing a series of commercials for the church back in the 1970s called *Home Front*. LeGrand Richards, one of the Apostles of our church who was overseeing the campaign, came over to me during a break and said, "Jay, you look a little worried about something." I told him what I was concerned about and he replied, "For every worry under the sun, there is a solution or there is none. Now, if there is one, hurry up and find it. But, if there isn't one, never mind it." I'll never forget him or that great saying he shared with me.

- One time I was at a Scout outing with one of my boys, and I pulled out a piece of paper to write a note to a friend. I wrote the letters PVBPSB on the note, and the person sitting next to me politely asked what those letters stood for. I told him that it was an acronym for my philosophy of life. Plan your life with vision, budget your money with prudence, and structure your time with balance. He seemed to like it and understand it, which made me happy. I have always held true to this formula in my life, and it works for me (I later put these letters on my license plate).

- The age of technology has its downfalls. Thanks to technology, our lives move at such a fast pace that oftentimes a little something can be lost in translation when we are depending on voice mails, emails and texting to do our talking. During 2009, when I was working on my solo CD, *It's About Time Again,* I was doing a lot of emailing and texting back and forth with Gaynor Brunson, my friend and coproducer/engineer for that project. Somewhere during that time, my son and I had a discussion via text, which got a little heated. We were going back and forth, and I finally sent him a text that said he needed to really grow up and not be so selfish. He needed to remember to extend an arm of fellowship to others and not be so self-centered. I said, "I love you man, and I'm there for you, but you really need to think about what I said." I hit send—and promptly sent it to Gaynor instead of my son. When I realized my error, I immediately got in touch with Gaynor to let him know about my mistake. Gaynor said, "Whew! I thought it was from one of my girlfriends!"

- On a lighter note, my brother Wayne has a beautiful living room in his house, and he goes there to feel peace and contentment, especially when he is bothered by something. He has a joke he sometimes uses in our shows: "If you ever feel like dying, go to the living room." People think he's joking, but there is actually something to that for him!

- One day I had a discussion with my boys about the popular phrase, "What would Jesus do?" In our home, we have a picture of the Savior with the quote from our prophet that I think better states the thought, "What would He have me do?" We love how that simple change in words puts a whole new light on that phrase.

FAVORITE QUOTES

The following are some great affirmations I've used that have helped me pull through many situations. They didn't really change the problem, but they changed the way I perceived the situation.

"If there is no solution, there is no problem."

"God answers knee-mail."

"We can't become what we want to be by remaining who we are."

"Tough situations can make us bitter or better—we have a choice."

"Sometimes God allows us to fall on our backs so that we look up."

"The Lord doesn't look at your ability, only your availability. If we prove our dependability, we will increase our capability."

"Faith requires one step at a time. We can't expect the Lord to guide our footsteps if we aren't willing to move our feet."

"Faith is to step into the darkness knowing that light will follow."

"May we never measure our lives by the days we have lived, but by the smiles we leave behind."

"Go and do, don't sit and stew."

"The church is a workshop for the sinners, not a museum for the saints."

"There are three kinds of people: those who make things happen, those who watch things happen, and those who wonder what happened."

"Discipline is remembering what you want."

"Treat others the way you would want to be treated."

"Forgive yourself, and you will forgive others."

"Actions speak louder than words."

"Put your own oxygen mask on first."

"We are human beings, not human doings."

"If you can see it, you can achieve it."

"Expect less and love more."

"The five secrets of a good marriage: Attention, Affection, Acceptance, Adoration, Appreciation."

"You can't change people—only your reaction to them."

"Habits are what shape our character."

"It's hard to be a positive person with a negative mind."

"Success is persistence and determination."

"Push back the pull of the world, and then you'll find peace."

"Life is a journey. Enjoy the ride."

"If the Lord seems far away, look and see who's moved."

"Under-promise and over-deliver."

"Happy is the person who has an attitude of gratitude."

"We are all children of God."

"Love thy neighbor as thyself."

"People don't care how much you know until they know how much you care."

"Plan your work, then work your plan."

"I see and I forget; I hear and I remember; I do and I understand."

Stage Notes

IT'S ALL RELATIVE

I have always been very close to my family, physically and emotionally. We have lived together, worked together, and laughed together for more than five decades. Following are my thoughts about my wonderful parents, brothers, and sister—and their memories about me.

My Wonderful Parents

My father had a different way of seeing the world. He had a keen sense of others. Father was very conscious of how people were feeling and could discern their moods, thoughts, and behaviors so well. He was a very successful salesman in his younger days (he could sell ice to the Eskimos). Father believed, "You can't change people—only your reaction to them." He was a very good man and everybody loved him. He was full of love, compassion, and integrity. My father loved the saying, "Do what is right, let the consequences follow." If I were to describe him in just a few words, I would say he was a man of great faith, who radiated love, kindness, honor, and dignity throughout his life.

My mother was also brilliant at looking at things differently and from different angles. She was a very positive person and lived her life "looking at the glass half full." My mother would turn lemons into lemonade and see the world through rose-colored glasses. I loved her for that. I also loved the way she'd help me when people did something to disappoint me. She had boundless love and forgiveness for others. Mother believed, "Scars are just tattoos with better stories." She believed that death was just a part of life, a change of scenery, and another thing we have to live through. Her quest for peace of mind and zest for life affected not only her family, but everyone she talked to. Mother loved fans and they loved her; in fact, many of them referred to her as "Mother." She posted many affirmations around our house when we were growing up. One in particular that really stuck out for me is one I've mentioned before: "Prepare yourself, and the opportunity will come." She was a scholar of the scriptures and believed intelligence was the wise application of knowledge. When my brothers and I got into fights and wanted her to take sides, she would respond with, "It takes two to tango." (You could say Donny took that literally when he won *Dancing with the Stars* in November 2009!)

A few days before my father lost his speech, I asked him what his thoughts were about dying. He said, "I miss Olive so much! But, I'm just now getting my family where they need to be."

Life, to my parents, was a journey and just another step to Eternity. They tried to prepare us for the trials that would eventually come, and I feel they succeeded. Their attitude toward adversity was what really made the difference for me. They understood the purpose of life and that the obstacles we faced were only opportunities to overcome and become better. Too many people let life's obstacles make them become bitter.

I will always be grateful for their teachings and love for the Gospel of Jesus Christ. They lived what they preached. They applied what they learned. There is a saying that reminds me of them: "The more we know, the more we do; and the more we do, the more we become." They loved everybody. I still feel their presence often. My parents had a little signal which we've continued using in our own families. They would squeeze our hands three times in a row, signifying the syllables for "I love you." This is my last memory of both of them before they passed away.

My Amazing Father, George

I called Father "ParPar" (because he was always "on par for the course") or "Dee Dah" (that's "Daddy" backwards). My father in turn had a nickname for me—"Knuckles," because I would always fumble things around.

I'll never forget the visit to see my father on May 1, 2006. Kandilyn, Jason, and I were visiting Father in the hospital. He was alert and aware of what was going on, and his memory was good. The only problem was that his speech had deteriorated to the point that it was hard to understand him. However, about halfway through a mumbled conversation, he stopped, grabbed my hand, and told Jason (just as clear as could be), "I want you to know how much I love your dad!" I couldn't hold back the tears and gave my father a kiss and a hug. That hug seemed to freeze-frame in my mind to something he said, and did, way back in time. I remember a specific time long ago when my father gave me a big, tight hug and said, "Never forget that." I have never forgotten. (That squeeze hug continued on in my family.)

I remember when my brother Jimmy, his son Zak, and I were visiting Father after Mother had passed away. He was feeling lonely. When it was time to leave, I gave him a kiss and told him how much I loved him. He said, "Well of course you do, because I'm full of love for you!" He then said, "I love you more, because I loved you first!"

My father once told me that the reason he didn't like retirement age was because many people feel as though they're "put out to pasture." He warned me that once this feeling sets in, a person begins to fall apart, loses purpose, and quickly dies inside. Up until the very end, my father kept himself busy and in the service of people. As my brother Tom said, he planned his work and worked his plan. My father not only endured to the end of life, he endured it well.

One day, when my father and I were walking together, and he stopped and said, "Jay, I hope I've been a good example to you. I hope that you remember the things that I did right and apply them in your life. I also hope you can look at the things I've done wrong and learn from them." Now that is humility! What a great example my father has been to me. My father has been gone for several years, but he used to tell the following story about me:

> *One time Jay was acting up, so I spanked him. I pointed my finger at him and said, "Jay, this is love." Then, I hugged him and said, "So is this." I always believed if I didn't teach Jay, society would. Discipline is a form of love, and it has been my job to train him the best I can. One time when Jason was little, Jay and I took him out to eat with us and we ended up getting in a little "money fight" over who would pay the tab. Jason watched on in frustration and finally settled things by saying, "Daddy! Mind your Daddy!" Out of the mouths of babes!*

> *—George Osmond*

Memories of My Mother, Olive

My nickname for my mother was "Angel," and I don't think any other nickname could have fit her better.

My mother was known for her wisdom and her use of inspirational quotations. Some of my favorites from her are "Do what is right; let the consequences follow"; "This too shall pass"; and "It is important to marry the one you love, but more important to love the one you marry." My mother had such vision!

I couldn't write this book without sharing an experience I had early in September 2005 while in England. It was a beautiful day in September. I was looking out the window, which had been opened slightly. The breeze was warm, the sun was shining through the clouds, and there were swan swimming in the lake across the road. I thought to myself, this is what heaven must be like. I felt a longing to have my family with me. Oh, how I missed them. I wanted them to experience this beautiful sight with me. I wished I could hold each of them in my arms for just a moment (though I was thankful I could be at my brother Jimmy's house with his sweet family; it took a lot of the sting away from missing my little family). Just then, a wonderful feeling came over me like I have never felt before. It was as though someone was present in the room with me—someone very familiar to me. It was almost as if time went backwards for a moment, and then forward. It is difficult to describe this, but I heard my mother's voice say to me, "Jay, now you know how I feel. I love you, Son." I know it is hard to believe, but I really did experience this amazing moment. Those who know me know that I'm not a spiritualist, and I don't even like to talk about strange things. But, this was a wonderful blessing that got me through many lonely times while I was there in England.

It was wonderful getting back to my family. There is nothing like those little arms (even though they're now big) around my neck. I know this is the very same feeling my mother is waiting for. I also know she is not up there taking it easy eating grapes. She is bringing glad tidings to many souls and working hard to teach people the Gospel. She was, and is, an inspiration to me. I have so much to thank her for, including my testimony of the wonderful Gospel of Jesus Christ!

When I was a teenager, my little mother gave me a plant one day after a long period of answering a thousand questions I had about the church. She wrote a note and put it with this plant, which said, "Jay, I enjoyed our conversation and the questions you have about the church. Here is something to help you along the way as you go throughout your life. I hope you think and ponder its significance. I love you and want more than anything to help you enjoy the peace that comes through having a testimony of the Gospel of Jesus Christ." The note continued,

> Just as this plant needs water to grow, so does your spirit need to drink every day, from the living well of the scriptures. This plant needs air to survive, and your

soul needs prayer to survive. If this plant doesn't get the proper nutrients from the soil, it will not blossom and develop. If you don't keep the commandments of God, you too will not enjoy life to its fullness. And finally, if this plant is deprived of the warmth of the sunlight, it will shrivel up and die. Our spirits crave light and knowledge from God. You need that warmth of the Holy Ghost to keep you safe, happy and strong. Look to our Savior, and live! Love, Mother.

Many people knew my mother, and those who did were surely blessed to be in her presence. She loved them and still does. She spent countless hours writing to and talking with many people about their lives and how they fit into God's great plan. My mother has passed on, but she would frequently tell the following stories about me to friends and family.

It was about 1970. We took the kids to the store because we needed to buy them all new beds. When it came time to choose a mattress, I said to Jay, "Now be sure to choose a good one. You'll be spending one third of your life sleeping on it." Jay thought about that for awhile, then said, "Mother, if the Lord lets us spend one third of our lives asleep, we really ought to be good the rest of the time!"

Jay used his imagination to turn hair clips into airplanes and such. We would be on the road traveling, and it wasn't really where Jay wanted to be at the time. So, he would escape into his imagination by playing with the hair clips. Looking back, I realized this was an adapter to stress for him. I also read once that the kind of child who will use his imagination like that has the most brilliant kind of mind there is. That's Jay!

—Olive Osmond

Virl, My Hero

I've often called Virl "Squirrel," I guess just because the two words rhyme, but I don't think he likes it too much. My brother Virl is the oldest child of the Osmond family. He is extremely talented, creative, and witty. He is also very intelligent. However, Virl has felt a lot of pressure being the first son. Not only is he a member of a family who is known for its singing, but he is also challenged with the tough reality of being hard of hearing. Virl has struggled to find his place in this family. He has felt responsible to keep the family together and to encourage us to keep on the straight and narrow path. He has felt alone many times and has perceived himself to be on the outside, because of the notoriety of his performing brothers. Virl has told me of the many trials he's had feeling like an outcast. He has also related to me a number of self-esteem problems that he has gone through because of his deafness. It is because of his desire to overcome obstacles, and his determination to succeed, that our mother was inspired to create the Osmond Foundation, which later became known as The Children's Miracle Network.

I love this guy! He is a champion in my eyes. I look up to Virl with respect as someone who has been through the refining fire. Not only is he a great example to me of how a person can endure trials well, but he also possesses the patience of Job and strives to incorporate the principles of love and kindness that were wonderfully exemplified by our Savior. Virl is my hero.

> *I love Jay so, because he makes me happy whenever he is around me. He is a man in whom there is no guile. He cheers me up when I am down. He makes me laugh and causes me to forget my trials and struggles in life. He is genuine and down-to-earth—a simple man. Jay finds joy in everything and has a great love and compassion for all of God's creatures. Throughout Jay's life, I have witnessed the love he has for all of our Father's Heavenly children. He is truly my special brother.*
>
> *—Virl Osmond*

The Joy of Being Tom's Brother

My brother Tommy (or "Turkey Tom") is probably the funniest of all my brothers. It is like he is always in "entertainment mode." I suppose Tom is not different—he probably feels like he was born to entertain like the rest of our family. However, due to his deafness, Tom never had his chance on stage. He is constantly entertaining people, feeling that life was meant to make people laugh, and lifting others. There are times when his mime and tap dancing routines can become a little irritating; but when I really take a look at Tom's world, a world of deafness, I find his exuberance is actually quite refreshing.

Tommy is very positive and deeply religious. The trials he's had to endure seem to have become his stepping stones for understanding and his purpose for life. Tommy lives a very quiet and predictable existence in rural Utah. I often find that somewhat enviable.

I remember this particular story about Jay from back when we were pretty young and living in Huntsville, Utah. My father demonstrated to my brothers and me how to shoot a rifle. This demonstration took place in the basement of the house that my father's brother, Ralph, built for us. The view from the north side of our house was of the fishing pond. Our father asked each one of the brothers to take a turn and said he loaded enough bullets for each of us to take one shot aimed at the fishing pond. When it was Jay's turn, he pulled the trigger and the bullet was shot; but then he kept pulling the trigger and shot several more times. Our father was really mad at him! I remember thinking how funny Jay was, getting carried away with his shots, so I giggled. To me, Jay just wanted to meet a new challenge and kept going for the best. Bless his heart! Jay has a tender heart and I love him very much.

—*Tom Osmond*

My Brother Alan, and Regrets

One of the hardest things I've had to accept is the fact that my brother Alan, who we called "Big Al," broke my nose. Not only did he break it, but it was considered "crushed," per my visit to the emergency room at the hospital in Indianapolis. The doctor on call said all he could do was shape and try to hold it in place; if that didn't work, I'd be looking at plastic surgery. He also indicated that if Alan had hit me just slightly higher, he would have pushed the bones up to my brain. Any lower, and I would have lost all my teeth.

Chuck Norris was a good friend; and since we were all taking karate from him at that time (and were halfway to being black belts), he thought it would be fun to create a fight and put it to music. Elvis really was the one who got us interested in karate. We wanted to be like him, and he influenced us towards the martial arts. (Those who have followed us have seen from our old videos the impact karate has had on our dancing.)

I can't believe I trusted my brother to come within micro-inches of my face. I wanted it to look as real as possible. So did he—obviously. I'll never forget that hot day on stage, looking out over thousands of faces, and then seeing Alan—super-charged—swinging his arm back. Then *walla-woom*—I saw red and then stars. Next, I saw Alan's face as I laid on the ground and heard him say, "Jay, I'm so sorry, please forgive me!" He must have said this five times—or at least it seemed. Everything went quiet for me, except for hearing Alan's voice.

As I was rushed downstairs to the dressing room, I saw myself in the mirror with a flat nose and blood. I thought about how just before the show, I was grooming my "fro" in that same mirror. I heard one of my brothers announce over the microphone, "Please give us a minute to have a prayer for Jay—we'll be right back." The first aid staff taped my nose to stop the bleeding (I looked ridiculous in the mirror—only I didn't notice my "fro" this time). I remember the blessing given to me as time seemed to stand still.

I remember saying to myself, "I can't disappoint these people, and the show must go on!"

The decision was mine as to whether I went to the emergency room right away or continued the show. Since we were pretty close to the end, I decided to stay and finish. I was (at that time in my life) in the mindset of "one for all, and all for one."

After the show, my nose felt like it exploded. Somehow I was blessed to feel numb while we finished the show. As I walked down the side stage stairs with two State Troopers, there was silence. I saw hundreds of faces in the backstage area with spellbound looks. I got into the patrol car and was rushed to the hospital. The pain really started then—it was excruciating, and they gave me medication to calm the intensity down.

That night was one of the worst nights of my life. I was really hurting—not just physically, but emotionally. The anger towards Alan didn't come until years later, but I could see the guilt on his face. "If only," were the words he'd try to say to me but couldn't; instead, he repeated over and over, "I'm so sorry Jay, please forgive me."

Those words stayed in my mind for years. Even though I pretended to forgive him, my heart was angry about the stupidity of both of us. Years later, I finally forgave him in my heart. I remember hugging him and shaking his right hand (that now limped because of his multiple sclerosis). I saw his knuckle that he fractured when he hit me, and I looked into his eyes and said, "I love ya buddy; I forgive you." I felt his pain, as mine drained out of me. I felt the love, sorrow, and compassion he must have felt for me as he responded back, "I love you too, brother."

I knew then that true forgiveness from me—finally—had been given. True peace was now in the place of resentment, hurt and anger.

I thank my God for giving us the power to truly love. So many of us carry malice and bitterness within, even after the person who has harmed us is truly sorry. I learned a great lesson through this. I learned that we all make mistakes and hurt others accidentally (or on purpose). Wouldn't it be great if we, when we have been hurt or offended, could be the first to extend a loving hand or warm embrace, and say the words, "I love you!" (p.s. One of the things that my wife said attracted her to me was my crooked septum bone in my nose. Lemons into Lemonade.)

I will never forget the feeling I had when I smashed Jay in the nose in Indianapolis, Indiana, and knocked him 15 feet into his own drum set. We were doing a karate fight routine that Chuck Norris staged with us.

We brothers always wanted to make our stage demonstrations look as realistic as possible, as though we were really hitting each other—and that day, it definitely was real. I was supposed to knee Jay in the stomach and then come around and hit him in the face with a round-house (pulling our punches, of course). Due to a little too much "energy" by me (probably due to brotherly competition over the years), and a little tardiness on Jay's part (probably because I knocked the wind out of him with my knee), fist met nose and there went the shows!

Actually, when I hit Jay, I thought I may have done him in. His nose sounded like a watermelon being split open with a knife. He was knocked into his drum set, and I had never known the meaning of rubber legs until I saw him trying to hold himself up. I told the audience of over 20,000 people to not go away and that we would be right back after we had a word of prayer. I didn't need to tell the audience that—it just came out. I just knew that we needed some divine help . . . and an ambulance.

My hand was dripping blood, while Jay's nose barely bled at all. We finished the karate fight, said goodnight to the audience, and ran off stage where two police squad cars were waiting to transport us to the emergency room. Just as soon as we told the audience goodbye, Jay's nose started bleeding profusely, so we were rushed out with sirens blasting. We had Jay's nose stitched up and my hand

*stitched up (cut by Jay's nose bones); and we went back and
did the second show 45 minutes later, including the karate
fight. After, we went back to the hospital, set Jay's nose
(which was broken in six places), and re-bandaged both of
our wounds.*

—Alan Osmond

Crazy Wayne

My brother Wayne has to be the ultimate character on the
planet. We don't affectionately call him "Crazy Wayne" for nothing.
We all have nicknames, but for some reason, Wayne seemed to
have several. Besides "Crazy Wayne," to me he is "Wayne-o,"
"Squeaker," and "Wings." Wayne was my roommate throughout
the 1960s and 70s. Wayne has taught me many lessons over the
years, some of which were patience, acceptance, tolerance, and the
ability to stay cool under fire. Over the years, I lived through two
hotel fires with Wayne, an earthquake, and girls banging on our
hotel room doors (we wouldn't let them out—just kidding!). As is
true with most siblings, there was a time when he used to get on
my nerves. Wayne would keep himself busy when we were on the
road by making arrows, bullets, and belts in our hotel rooms. Can
you imagine trying to sleep with all the ruckus of Wayne's creativity
going on? But one day I realized the world would not be the same
without him. Because of my change in perception, my love for
him grew. This is a good example to me of the "glass half empty
or half full" concept. Our attitudes shape the way we view others
and accept them. I feel when we try to look at things differently,
we practice acceptance. I really believe there are things we can learn
and love about everyone and everything.

Wayne is actually a very serious dude, and that is what makes
him so funny. You have to know him to really understand what I'm
trying to say. My world wouldn't be the same without Wayne.

*When Jay was a little boy, we used to travel to Salt
Lake City from Ogden, often several times a week. We all*

*traveled in a big, dark green van with white lines that we
called "Mugsy." These trips would take at least an hour each
way. Jay would always sit in the back seat of Mugsy and
play his imaginary games. He always had two silver hair
clips with him, which would become airplanes or rockets.
He also made his own sound effects. I always wondered
exactly what he was doing, but he would entertain himself
the whole way. Jay would put the hair clips in his pocket
and take them everywhere we went. Whether it was just
a free minute or a little extra time to fill, he would take
them out of his pocket and play with those two hair clips—
while we were blocking on stage or waiting in a line, etc.
He was never bored like the rest of us.*

*Jay is a wonderful brother and a good friend. Love
you, Bro.*

—Wayne Osmond

My Bond with Merrill

My brother Merrill (whom we call "Bear") grew up side-by-side with me. He and I have been through everything together and sometimes laugh about it all. All we have to do is look at each other, and we know what the other is thinking. Growing up in a close family and working hard together can either bond us or create a desire to avoid each other. Merrill and I have a strong bond, and it has stayed in tact over the years. We have had to create some space from each other, because our lives were so intermingled. Merrill and I are both very right-brained, creative people who lack a desire for detail. This has gotten us into trouble many times, because we tend to skip the attention that is needed to accomplish tasks. We've been able to rally others to come to our aid, which is both good and bad. We have become so dependent on that aid that we are kind of caught in a rut of codependency. We are trying very hard to change that habit. If you'll notice, as I write about my thoughts regarding Merrill, I use the group mentality of "we." This is because we were raised like Marines: the "one for all, and all for one" school of thought. Merrill has managed to go it alone in show business a lot better than I have. I have had my spurts of independency in other areas of life, but not in this business. It's too difficult and challenging to brave it alone; and as I've always said, I truly believe deep down inside that we are better and stronger together than on our own. Merrill is a brother who has been blessed with the talent of persuasion. Like our father, he could literally sell ice to the Eskimos. He has the quality of sincerity (which truly is sincere) that melts people to think things his way. Merrill is a good man, and his heart is in the right place. The only flaws he really has are that he is too trusting and too dependent. Those are two flaws I can very much relate to.

> *It is virtually impossible for me to write, in a paragraph or two, my thoughts regarding my brother Jay. Fifty years standing by his side has been more than a blessing to my life—it has given me a lifetime worth of memories that will remain with me for eternity. His trials, along with his personal moments of joy, have brought those that know him a depth of understanding regarding sacrifice that goes beyond my comprehension. To know my brother Jay is to know a Christ-like love that knows no bounds. Jay has no guile or ego. He is truly a man of pure integrity. I love my brother.*

> *—Merrill Osmond*

Donny: My Brother the Star

My brother Donny (whom I call "D-ber"), is a very smart individual. He has always been technically smart and very left-brained. He's always been able to calculate numbers and concepts quickly without even writing them down. At age 10, Donny built a radio. At age 13, he designed a motorized apparatus that was able to move his bed up and down on an elevator shaft to expose his laboratory beneath. Donny has also had a very strange adolescent life. I remember going with Donny to see a bunch of girls who were rehearsing a cheerleading routine at Provo High School in Utah. Suddenly, a bunch of teenage boys came around the corner with rocks and cans and started throwing them at us. This was a typical event in the life of my brother Donny when we were growing up, so he became a loner. Those were very difficult times for Donny; girls loved him, and guys hated him. Everyone knows my brother. Donny has been popular since the beginning of his life, but nobody knows the challenges that popularity brought to him. I sort of know and can attest that his life has not been easy. He and I have had some major talks about all this stardom and popularity. Believe me, it's not what people think it is; there is a lot of pressure to maintain, to perform, and to always be good.

When someone has that level of popularity, we have to try to look at him or her as more than an entertainer and remember there is a real individual there when the "celebrity" is set aside. That real person is just like everybody else, with the same hopes and dreams, problems, and fears as the rest of us. But you see, that leaves two identities to deal with, and that is not easy. I've written about the time when "Donny the entertainer" and "Donny the person" were at odds with each other. The wonderful thing is that they now seem to have joined together. I'm not saying Donny has a split personality; what I do mean is that he beat the struggle of putting "Donny the person" and "Donny the superstar" into one person.

I remember when Jay taught me how to ride a bicycle. I was seven years old and Jay was nine. It was on an old red Schwinn. As he was teaching me, he let me fall into a ditch and right into some barbed wire. Thanks a lot, Jay!

Another memory I have is how Jay always entertained himself by playing with hair clips. He had a great imagination. Jay could see people and things in these hair clips as he bent them into various shapes. I always wished I had that kind of imagination.

I remember the banana tree in Arleta. Jay, Jimmy, Marie, and I pretended we were spies. We had our base on the veranda of the house and would slide down this banana tree from the "base" to the ground two stories below. We would all do it, including Marie. I remember one time when Jay tried to do it, he panicked and didn't slide. He just hung there. Finally his weight overpowered the tree. The tree broke and down came Jay. I'll never forget the look on Jay's face.

Another memory was when we experienced an earthquake. Jay and I shared a room at that time. The whole house was shaking, and things were falling. I was sleeping on the bunk bed, and Jay was lying on the bed across the room. I remember seeing Jay lift his head up. Just as he did, a heavy metal Chinese head fell from the wall and landed right on Jay's pillow. His head had been there only a fraction of a second earlier. The experience was both amazing and terrifying.

—Donny Osmond

Marie, My Little Sis

My little sister, Marie, is a wonderful person. I call her "Sis" or "Little Sis." She has a deep sense of compassion for others and is very religious; but as the world knows, Marie has had a very unusual life. As a little girl, she had a hard time adjusting to being the only girl in a family with eight brothers. She was first a "tomboy" and tried to fit in with the rest of us but struggled to find her place. Marie and I were at odds a lot of the time when we were kids. She would do things to bug me, and in return I would say something mean. I also used to tease her relentlessly and drive her crazy (I know, it doesn't sound like me, but it's true). So, Marie and I weren't close as kids. When Marie was about 13, she started to really come alive. And once I grew up, I apologized for my big brother antics. I then started to treat her like the lady she had become. Marie recorded her first song, "Paper Roses," and finally felt that she made a strong identity statement of her own. My little sis went from being a tomboy to this sweet little gal. It actually shocked me! I never saw such a transformation in a person. The more time went on, the more confident she became. Through the years, and all of the tests and trials that came with them, Marie developed a hard shell to protect herself from getting hurt. She was still very sweet and nice but somewhat distant. Today, my little sis is a well-seasoned, successful, and mature woman, who has been through many changes and tough times. To me, she will always be my little, sweet, sensitive sis who is really very shy and just a little unsure of what the world holds next for her. I love her!

My brother Jay is a dedicated family man and would face any amount of danger for his wife and children, siblings, or nephews and nieces. But there is one thing he is acutely afraid of . . . moths!

There was an incident when Jay was about eight years old, in which he felt a tickle behind his ear that forever changed his perspective on the dreaded Animalia Arthropoda Insecta Lepidoptera (which is the scientific word for "moth"). Thinking it was just an itch, he went to scratch it and squished a huge moth against his head. I guess the resulting insect blood and guts were much more disturbing to Jay than anyone ever knew. We found out the truth about ten years later.

The family was touring in Malaysia and doing a show at the Genting Highlands Resort. Our hotel rooms were on a high floor near where the neon signs were hung on the outside of the building. When we got there, someone went to pull open the curtains so we could see the nighttime view. About two dozen moths flew from the window into the room. Suddenly, there was a loud shriek behind me, and then I heard the sound of footsteps running and a door slamming. It was my sweet brother Jay, fleeing the group of terrifying predators.

*I love my brother Jay, so I will never ask him to stand
and talk to me on the front walk to my house at night with
the porch light on. That would be mean. In fact, I think
I'll send him a box of mothballs for Christmas this year.*

—*Marie Osmond*

We had to leave quickly after the show in Malaysia, because insurgents were penetrating the area (this was during the Vietnam War). They sent escorts to take us down the mountain without lights and get us into helicopters for departure. With all of this chaos going on, I wasn't as concerned about the communists in the area as I was about the moths!

Jimmy, My Buddy

My youngest brother Jimmy has always been my little pal. I often call him "Jimper," "Monkey," "Chimp," "Jimmer," or "Jimp." He and I have stuck really close together through the years and have supported each other through thick and thin. When I think of my little brother, the lyrics from the song, "Together, Wherever We Go," say it all: "Wherever we go, whatever we do, we're gonna go through it together."

Looking back over the many thousands of pictures I sorted through for our 50th anniversary special, you could see the love and the bond Jimmy and I have.

Jimmy grew up the hard way. I have such respect for him. He has faced obstacles that the rest of of us haven't had to. His leadership in our family has been with love and kindness. Jimmy's integrity is one of his many strengths. Jimmy has taken on several career challenges over the years—he produced and promoted record-breaking worldwide concert tours, starred in various stage productions such as *Grease* and *Chicago*, had four number one records in the U.K. (including "Long-Haired Lover from Liverpool"), appeared on the highly rated British television program, *I'm a Celebrity, Get Me Out of Here!*, and even learned to sing opera when he appeared on the U.K. television program, *Popstar to Operastar.*

Jimmy is a talent beyond belief, a character beyond imagination, and a brother beyond words. To know him is to love him.

When we were younger, Jay was always concerned if I was having enough fun, if I was getting enough exercise, and if I had enough friends. He decided to take it upon himself to be my best friend, which he still is. He would take me golfing, play football with me, help me meet people, help me with my spelling, attend some of my baseball games, and be there whenever something important was going on in my life. I have great memories of going to the golf course with Jay. We'd each have a chocolate shake in hand and listen to our favorite songs on the radio. In a funny but sarcastic way, we would always tell each other what we thought the other was doing wrong with his golf swing.

One particular day, we were at Cascade Golf Course, hole 8 (a par 4). It was a very steep hill down to the green, and it had rained the night before. The grass was still wet. I guess we both had bad shots, so naturally we started in on each other. We hopped into the golf cart and started down the steep hill. I was driving and was going super fast. The cart slipped sideways on the wet grass and spun around three or four times before Jay flew out and I ran over him with the cart!

We laughed our heads off—and from that time forward, we stopped giving each other golf lessons. This is just one of the many fun times I remember spending with my brother Jay. He has always been a great example to me. I love you, Jay,

—James Osmond

KANDILYN AND COMPANY

My nickname for Kandilyn is "Kandle-light." I have always joked that the nickname came from her telling people I have a night light (it's in the refrigerator door). But, I could also say it comes from the fact that when she walks into a room it lights up. Either way, she is my Kandle-light.

Marrying Kandilyn was the best thing I ever did. Not only did she light up my life, but she also brought into my life many people whom I love and adore—my children and my wife's side of the family.

Kandilyn

Kandilyn is an amazing person. She has struggled with shyness ever since she was a little girl—but when you meet her, that is hard to believe. When my family kicked off the celebration of our 50th anniversary in entertainment, Kandi really saved the day. We had several events planned around the concerts we were performing at The Orleans in Las Vegas (these events were being filmed for our PBS Special). One of the events was called, "Jay's Film Fest," which was an idea that came from all the video footage we were going through to prepare for the television special.

Obviously, not all of that memorable old footage could be used for the special, so I got the idea to put some of it together and have a special showing for our fans that were there. There was a lot of media coverage surrounding these events; and unfortunately, I got tied up with interviews when my film fest was supposed to be taking place. Rather than canceling and disappointing people, Kandi took my place as host and narrator of "Jay's Film Fest." She dazzled people with her ability to be funny and interesting as she "color commentated" the video footage with stories and memories. I still have fans approach me and remark how great Kandi was that day, and you can't imagine what a huge step that was outside of her comfort zone. Being funny and interesting are two characteristics that have always been present in our marriage; there is never a dull moment with Kandi. As someone who battles depression and general anxiety, as well as social phobia, the way Kandi lives life despite those challenges amazes me. The fact that she can still deal with me is amazing in itself! Kandi is truly a saint, a wonderful wife, and a great mom.

"What is it like to be married to an Osmond?" That is the question I'm most often asked. I suppose I could answer by saying, "What is it like to be married to a Jones, or a Thomas, or even a Harris?" Every person and every experience is completely unique, so how can I give an adequate answer? When someone asks me that question, they are simply wondering if my life is really all that different than theirs. I suppose the truly honest answer is yes and no.

My husband loves me and our children. He works hard to provide for us. He has ups and downs, triumphs and heartaches, health and sickness. In truth, Jay is like anyone else, and yet Jay Osmond could never be described as "like anyone else." No one who truly knows Jay would ever describe him as an ordinary guy, and yet he is also incredibly down to earth. I think it has more to do with who Jay is than what he does. If he hadn't begun performing at the age of two, what would he be like today? Because Jay's life experiences have been so extraordinary, that's a fair question. Our experiences help define who we are. Certain skills are learned through certain experiences. Jay has had to learn to deal with situations that most people would never even have to think about—situations like meeting royalty and world leaders; performing flawlessly while having the flu or a shattered nose; and traveling around the world numerous times while personally greeting millions of fans. Although these experiences and countless others have shaped who he is, I admire Jay's ability to remain generally unaffected. I feel Jay is such a generous, thoughtful, extremely kind, and fun-loving man. People are always telling me that they are surprised when they meet Jay. I suppose that's because we expect people who live "in the public eye" to look and act a certain way. Being with Jay has helped me learn to reserve judgment with everyone I meet.

By the time this book is published, Jay and I will have been married for 23 years. Since I was married at the age of 20, I can say that I've now been an Osmond longer than I was a Harris. My perception of the world has changed over that amount of time. I can still remember the shock I felt on my first date with Jay when people in the restaurant stopped, stared, and began whispering as he and I were led to our table. Jay was completely unaware that anything unusual was even happening. He has never known any other reaction. Although I'm still aware of the extra attention we receive, I now understand where it is coming from and can appreciate it for what it is. Although I would still prefer to be incognito and have my husband all to myself, I realize that the amount of attention Jay receives is a tribute to the hard work, integrity, professionalism, and talent that he and his family have exhibited over the past 50-plus years. How can anyone complain about that?

Stepping into his world was both frightening and thrilling for me. The adjustment was not an easy one. My life experiences, in many ways, had been very different from Jay's. I was a very shy person by nature. I liked some attention, but not too much of it. I remember the very first time someone asked me for my autograph. I felt flattered and bewildered at the same time and wanted to just blurt out, "Why?" I guess I didn't think that simply marrying someone famous was reason enough to warrant the personal attention of people I didn't know. I understood when someone wanted Jay's autograph, but mine? Why would anyone want my autograph? It was an inner battle that I would fight for more than two decades before finally finding peace with it.

I'll never forget one particular day. After being stopped by a group of people who wanted to talk to, take pictures with, hug, kiss, and get autographs from Jay, a woman in the group said to me, "Thank you for sharing your husband with us. I'm sure it can't be easy!" Her comment touched my heart and became the beginning of an understanding that, 20 years later, I now share with them.

She's right. "Sharing" your husband isn't easy. He is on the road approximately 75 percent of the year. The time I have with him is golden and precious to me. For the sake of our children, we have chosen to live in one place while Jay travels for his job. Occasionally we get to go with him (which has created amazing memories for our family), but for the most part the kids and I live a traditional life at home. I look forward to the day that I can travel with him year-round, but until then I treasure the times that he is home with us and the times when I get to rendezvous with him in various parts of the globe. Those rendezvous keep our marriage alive and help to counteract the loneliness. It is during those trips that I have to be patient, because I want his attention, too!

Jay is a wonderful man, and that's why I married him. He has all of the qualities I could possibly dream of and more in a husband. He is kind, attentive, hard working, funny, thoughtful, loving, clever, imaginative, determined, patient, and understanding. He is a man of great integrity. He is a worthy example for our sons of how a man should conduct his life. He is also a living example of how a man should treat his wife.

We have been blessed with three incredible sons and many amazing experiences. We have had numerous one-of-a-kind moments. It has been, and continues to be, an incredible journey.

—Kandilyn Osmond

Jason

Our son Jason (we had considered spelling his name "Jayson") was thought about many, many times before he was born. A dad could only hope to have a son like Jason (or as I call him—Jacer-Racer or Race Dog). When he was born, I was so anxious, excited, and nervous that I studied him over and over before the nurse came to take him to the nursery. I was so afraid that he would be mixed up with other babies (I'd heard nightmare stories about this). I couldn't believe I actually changed a diaper. He was my baby boy, and I was (and still am) so very proud of him.

Jason has always been there for me. I needed his companionship very badly one day, which happened to be my 35th birthday. Jason was two years old. For some reason that year, no one seemed to remember my birthday (or at least I didn't think they did) except for little Jason. Kandilyn was very sick, and most of the family was out of town. Jason came up to me with that priceless grin of his and said, "Happy Birthday, Dad!" Wow, that was just what I needed. We then proceeded to have probably one of the best birthdays of my life. We played racquetball at the Sherwood Hills Racquet Club (which we owned at the time), went to lunch and had ice cream—which he got in his hair and all over his face and clothes. I took him for his picture at Kiddie Kandids in the mall (which they later used in their main display). We bought toys, laughed and played, sang songs, hugged, told stories; and later he rode my shoulders and pulled my hair on a long and happy walk together. I will never forget that day! Children are great teachers of the joy of life!

Jason has always been a good boy and a very inquisitive kid. He also is very kinesthetic. He has to touch or taste everything. One day, I was telling him a story about Grandpa Osmond and how he was stranded up in the mountains as a kid. He was lost for three days, and no one could find him. I then told him that Grandpa had to survive by eating crickets and grasshoppers, etc. I could tell that hearing about this was fascinating to Jason. The next day, his counselor called me from school and said that Jason was in his office for bad behavior. That didn't sound like Jason at all, and I asked the counselor what he had done. The counselor said he was teaching the other kids to eat bugs. Now *that* sounded like Jason, and we had a good laugh.

Jason was always, and still is, a tease. Kandi and I used to play "hide and seek" with him. He would love to hide, and we would know where, but we'd pretend we didn't. We would say, "Where's Jason?" One day, Kandilyn thought I was watching Jason, and I thought she had him with her. Later that afternoon, we both came home and asked each other where Jason was. At that moment, a terrible panic hit us both. Neighbors joined us in an all-out search with no results. In tears, I was about to pick up the phone to call the police, when suddenly from the top of the refrigerator and out of the cupboard Jason jumped down. He said, "Daaad, did I scare you?!" Ever since that day, Kandi's nickname for him has been "Little Twerp."

Jason has always had a funny sense of humor. One time, when he was about eight years old, he was with me on a cruise. He really wanted to get a present for his mom from one of the cruise ship's shops. I told him to pick out two bracelet charms in the jewelry store. He chose an angel and a bear. When we got home, he asked if he could take them to "Show and Tell" at school before he gave them to his mom. I said, "Sure!" Jason's teacher, who was also a friend of ours, told us that when it came to his turn, he said, "There are two things this bracelet represents about my mom. The first thing is this little angel, because my mom is so sweet. The other is a bear, because you don't want to tick her off!"

Jason has such a wonderful attitude about life. I remember feeling down about traveling so much and being away from our family. He said, "Dad, just think about the Mormon pioneers who were kicked out of their homes and had to travel by wagon to Utah. You don't have it as bad as they did!"

It's hard not to sound like a proud parent when I talk about Jason. He is the first to admit he's not perfect, and he feels pressure when we make him sound like he is. However, if there is anyone on this earth who is striving to be better, to overcome life's challenges, and to help others with a kind word, a helping hand, or that big, wonderful smile, it's our Jason!

When my father first told me he was writing a book, my initial reaction was to laugh. Not because I didn't think he was serious; nor did I doubt he could do it. I laughed because it sounded like my dad had finally hit his stopping block, his pinnacle; he had reached the point where you sit down and go over everything that has happened in your life. Yep, it sounded like Dad was finally admitting he was old! But, after sitting down and thinking about it, I realized, "wait a minute . . . this is Dad we are talking about here! The ever-going, project after project, fun-loving man who raised me; this man could never get old. Nothing is going to stop him." So you never know . . . this very well may be the first of many books to come.

Now, when I was asked to put in a couple of my own words about Dad, my mind became flooded with so many things. I realized how much I respect my father and how much he really means to me. I realized how much he has taught me and how dumb I was the times I didn't listen. I realized he has accomplished so much and has experienced life in a way I cannot even begin to fathom. It amazes me how he was able to stay so close to his family and morals, having been thrust into the world's wildest business at the age of two. My father is, was, and always will be a rarity among men.

The single most important thing to my father is his family. I know it, and can say this is true, because throughout the years I have been alive, I have never once seen him put his needs or wants before my mother's or any of his children. That is such an example to my two younger brothers and me. He has taught me how to be a man. He has shown me how to be a father. He has taught me how to love a wife and to put her on the highest pedestal. Of course, my parents have been through hard times, but who hasn't? But, I can tell you he loves that woman more than life itself, and he will forever, into the eternities. My father tells us he loves us every day. I always assure him by saying, "I love you too, Dad," but then he always comes back saying, "Well, I love you more." Then I argue with him that he doesn't. Arguing always seems useless, because he always ends up winning. I think he really does love me more than I will ever know.

I have seen my father sacrifice, and sacrifice, and sacrifice again for me or for someone else's benefit. He loves unconditionally without hesitation—not only his family, but everyone. He is the guy who pulls over to help you if he sees you broken down on the side of a highway. He is the guy who picks up your $20 bill that you dropped and runs it over to you right before you get into your car. He is the guy who actually calls the number on the lost dog's collar tag to get it safely back to its owner. When I was younger, these random acts of kindness somewhat embarrassed me, because it was out of the norm. I was afraid, because I didn't understand. Now that I'm older, I can see how much of a difference someone like my father can make in *the world. He is a man who goes out of his way to help; and that, to me, is the best example of all.*

When it all comes down to it, I think my father is who he is, because he has a real relationship with his Heavenly Father, and he knows that Jesus Christ lives and is our Savior. I know he knows it, because I see it in him every day. His happiness comes from knowing he is a child of God and from teaching that knowledge to others. Although it might seem trite to some, it is what saves him and us, his family. My father is my hero, my example, and my best friend. One day I hope to be the person he has worked to teach me to be.

—Jason Osmond

Eric

Our second-born son, Eric, has been a very special blessing to Kandilyn and me. From the day he was born, we knew he would view things differently. He has brought a new perspective and love into our hearts. My little names for Eric are "Indigo" or "Eco."

The challenges that Eric has encountered are unique and quite out of the norm. He questions everything and has internally been at war with his thoughts. Because of this, he has learned to overcome negative thinking (which some might refer to as "demons") and has placed a high value on being true to one's self.

I have learned from Eric to not judge others harshly and to be socially compassionate. I used to look at teenagers who seemed poised for trouble in a different light. I now look at troubled youth as wonderful souls searching for answers to their problems. Instead of being critical of someone, I now say, "That's someone's Jason, Eric, or Marcus."

Eric has taught me so much about how important it is to be nice to ourselves. We can be so critical of ourselves, and in turn look critically at others. The Savior said, "Love thy neighbor as thyself." This is so true; and thanks to my son Eric, I have learned this lesson.

I'll never forget the time Eric and I were driving home from Missouri. We were in Lincoln, Nebraska. We had just finished watching a movie called, *The Day the Earth Stood Still.* Watching the movie got us into a discussion centered on religion. Eric and I had been at odds on some issues, and a heated discussion commenced (he loves to debate and is good at it; in fact, he is so good at it that he angered me). I became so frustrated that the volume of my voice started to increase, as did contention between us. I could tell that no matter what I said, he was going to take issue. Just as we were both about to yell, we looked down at the dashboard clock as it turned to 9:11. It was quite a reminder of what real disaster was, and we looked at each other, laughing over how silly we were being. A healthy spirit returned, and we both became more rational. I'm always learning something from Eric, and I love him very much. I am so thankful for him—and he will always be the "bright spot" in my life.

What's it like to be the son of Jay Osmond? Well, I'll tell you, it's an adventure. He's so spontaneous! Every single day is something new. He does everything, from catapulting water balloons across the park to fighting off a thousand hornets in the backyard; from shooting air-soft guns (with safety glasses of course) to driving RC cars; from writing/recording new music to ordering pizza and wheat burritos. Then, after we're all done, tired, and want to go home, he'll top it off by offering a bribe to go see the latest silly movie with him—with a big box of popcorn and a treat. Can you believe this guy? And yeah, he can fit it all into just one day!

It was when my dad would introduce himself as "Eric's crazy dad" that my friends would fall in love with the man and call him by their own little nicknames —like "Dad" or "Fazsha"—or the most popular, "Uncle Jay."

I've got my own little nicknames for him. Starting from the top: Pop, Popo, Fropo-Dropo, Papa, Fropsie, Dropsie, Fropazoid, Paparazzi, Popsicle, Dad, Dado, Dadio, Papa-Jay, Daddy (that was my first one), Padje, or just how I usually introduce him, "See this awesome guy right here? Yup, this is my dad!"

My Pop never likes to travel alone. Even though he's usually got his brothers with him, he says it's not the same without his "little family." (In case you didn't know, we are the smallest Osmond family there is.) So, when my dad has a trip coming up, he says, "Hey! I'm leaving to go to (fill in the blank). Who wants to come with me!?" Ha! He's so funny!

Speaking of funny, has he ever told you one of his jokes? His jokes are hilarious! He'll tell you the corniest joke, and then after the awkward silence . . . he starts cracking up at his own joke! It's not like a normal chuckle; it is his signature chuckle. So, the joke may even be just a little funny, but it becomes hilarious when he starts laughing at it, himself.

Another thing about my dad is his generosity. He's always willing to help someone out (no matter who they are). He'll drop everything just to help someone, and almost never thinks of himself. He is so caring. It seems that he gets along with everyone; and if he doesn't, he goes through the extra effort to become his or her friend. I'm telling you, he's genuine.

As a father, he possesses all the characteristics (and then some) of the ideal father. Yet, he's nowhere near perfect, as he keeps reminding us (but I've always felt that he's up there). With a man being so positive, encouraging, loving, enthusiastic, and spiritual, it's hard not to feel the same way. I am blessed to be his favorite second son and just one of three that will have the honor of continuing the Jay Osmond legacy. I sure do love my dad.

—Eric C. Osmond

Marcus

It was September of 1995. Kandi and I were upstairs in the toy room cleaning up, and she said, "There is something special about this child." I didn't know the meaning of that until my buddy Marc kicked his way into this world on January 8, 1996 (also Elvis Presley's birthday). "Mook" or "Marko," as I call him, has always wanted things to happen faster than they are supposed to. He is way beyond his years in maturity; in fact, sometimes I have to remind myself that he is still a kid. He has always tested the boundaries. Even as a baby, Marcus loved to pull the plug out on the vacuum when it was on, then run!

He constantly asks questions, then re-asks them with a different slant. Marc's impatience grew to become his strength when he invited me to go to Scout camp with him. He was considered the top expert "marksman" (no pun intended) with a rifle, the leader of his group of Scouts, and the one that endured to the end. He was also given an award at the end of Scout camp by our ward—for dealing with me! I thought I was tough in the snow, until the temperature went 10 degrees below zero. I realized I was not prepared for that kind of cold and went into a quiet panic. I began moaning and groaning about the situation to Marc, as well as to the whole troop. Night came, they still couldn't thaw me out, and everything I brought with me was frozen. That night, I actually thought I was going to get frostbite and die. Marc said, "Dad, you are going to be ok. Trust me." He then calmly tried to warm me up and talked me through the night. Marc said a vocal prayer (which I'm sure was heard by the camp, and for sure heard in heaven). In the morning after breakfast, Marcus said all I needed was a little faith. He said something else that I will never forget: "Life is like a Scout camp. We have to go through trials, earn some badges, and make it through. It's not easy, but it's worth it." (Where have I heard that before?)

The camp group decided it would be better to leave all the things I brought inside the tent and drag the whole thing two miles down the mountain to the base camp. That was the longest two miles I could have ever imagined.

Marc's deep sense of spirituality and understanding of the purpose of life has helped me to learn to be a better father. As I've said before, it is often the parents who are being taught.

To describe what it is like being the son of Jay Osmond is like describing the Declaration of Independence in one sentence: you just can't put it all into words. But, I will try. I cannot begin to tell you how amazing my father is. He is the perfect example of what a father, husband, role model, friend, and leader should be. I am eternally blessed with the presence of this phenomenal person. Whenever I am down, depressed, or have questions, he is always there. He often says to me, "I don't care if it is three o'clock in the morning. You can call me anytime!" He is a hard worker who still has time for his family and for his fans.

—Marcus Osmond

My Father-in-Law, Clint

My father-in-law is a great man. Kandi's parents have lived very close to us ever since we've moved back to Utah, and "Grandpa" is always available to help with projects when I need him. When we were first married, I asked him if he had any marital advice for me, since he knew Kandilyn better than anyone. He said, "Yes, just do what you're told." I've had a lot of fun with the Harris side of my family over the years, and they are really good about making sure I feel welcome whenever I visit. I'll always be grateful for the way Kandi was raised—they guided her to become the wonderful woman she is today.

Since returning to Utah and its colder climate after an 18-year stay in Southern California, we (the Harrises) have been rather avid snowmobile enthusiasts (mostly to have something to look forward to during the deep winter months). After a few years passed, the Osmonds also came back from Branson. Assuming they would enjoy a good snowmobile ride (we had three machines to share), we extended an occasional invitation to Jay, Kandilyn, and the boys to join us. We usually go to an area near Strawberry Reservoir (about two hours from home). It is quite open and reasonably flat, so we can keep an eye on the machines and riders in case a problem should arise. Needless to say, the boys always have a great time. We take a nice big lunch and try to pick a clear day with a lot of beautiful winter sunshine (this not only makes for a more pleasant outing, but also improves vision considerably and hence reduces the probability of an accident caused by poor visibility). Kandilyn isn't too excited about these activities but is a good sport, and Jay wears his big Osmond smile most of the time.

After one of these expeditions, we were all surprised when Jay announced he had the best time ever. Upon questioning as to why this time was so great, he admitted that he had finally been warm that day. It turned out that Kandilyn purchased him a good pair of insulated bibbed pants, which he donned for the first time, and finally stayed warm the whole day. On the other occasions he apparently was so cold and miserable, he had to fake that he was having fun. After all, the show must go on!

—Clint Harris (My Father-in-Law)

My Mother-in-Law, Kathy

Mother-in-law jokes have been told forever, but I'm very lucky to have a gem of a mother-in-law. Kandi and her mother are like best friends, and it is great to see the two of them have so much fun together. It has been a blessing to have Kandi's parents live so close, and my mother-in-law has always been able to help out with the kids and the pets when Kandi and I have had to travel. It is also a comfort to me to know that "Grandma" and "Grandpa," as I refer to them, are there to check in on my little family when I have to be on the road.

I will always cherish the memories that Clint and I had with Jay on the cruise that we took with him. How many young men would take their in-laws on a trip with them—especially, how many would take them on a cruise?

Kandilyn was not able to go with us, but that didn't stop Jay from taking us along. It was a beautiful ship, very elegant and the last time it would sail. He spent time with us, ate a lot of meals with us, and made us feel very important. He also let Clint and me have the only suite that was given to the Osmonds on that cruise. We love Jay and appreciate his kindness and generosity.

Jay is very protective and concerned for his family. His children and his wife are top priority in his life. They live in a nice, quiet neighborhood on a cul-de-sac. One day, as my husband and I were driving over to see Kandilyn and Jay, we saw large, plastic fluorescent men positioned every 100 or so feet along the roadway and cul-de-sac to their home. We instantly knew that these brightly colored safety figures were Jay's doing. He wanted everyone to slow down and drive carefully because there were children playing in the neighborhood. Jay doesn't just talk about doing things for safety, he jumps on the bandwagon!

Jay is an "otter." He loves to get the party going and then go take a nap. Jay is thrilled when everyone is having a good time. He spends a lot of time and money buying toys to help a party be successful. He would buy Marcus a croquet set and then say, "Grandma, wouldn't you like to teach Marcus how to play this game?" Jay is happiest when everyone else is happy. He is a definite treasure. Kites are one of Jay's favorite fun things to do. I wonder how many kites he has sent sailing away?

I love you, Jay, and I'm so glad that you are in our family.

—Kathy Harris (My Mother-in-Law)

Rob and Luz

Rob is a great guy—I really lucked out in the in-law department. Rob and his family live in southern Arizona, so we don't get to see them as often, but it is always great when we are able to all get together.

I've always had fun practicing my Spanish with Luz, and she's always been very patient when I do. She's such a good mother and really fun to be around.

It was around July of 2001. We just purchased a jet boat about two weeks prior, and Kandi called to let us know they would be coming to stay a few days before heading off to Disneyland. Of course, we had to go to the lake to let Jay's boys wakeboard and waterski. I remember the thermometer in the car showing 112 degrees. Obviously, with that kind of heat, the water was very comfortable. It was so hot that even Jay had to get in the water with us. I remember him saying more than once, "Wow, you can't even buy this much fun. This is just priceless!"

We all got into the boat to go for a ride. Jay watched his very athletic boys wakeboard, ski, and ride in the tube. The tube was about five feet around and had a bottom to it with a canvas cover surrounding it. Four small kids fit into it easily. Most people would sit or kneel in the bottom and hold onto the handles. After watching the kids do this for awhile, Jay said he would like to give tubing a try. Kandi agreed to join him in the tube.

We got them into the tube and took off slowly. You could tell they both were enjoying themselves by their big grins and bulging eyes. I began to speed up enough that the tube would hydroplane and I could turn and slide them over the wake. At about the same time, Jay decided to sit up on the side of the tube, which I think he assumed would be firmer than it was. At first it worked, and he sat on the edge with his hands straight up above his head. Next, he decided to lean backwards and put his hands in the water. This was when the tube slid off the edge of the wake. Jay flipped off the tube and went into a backwards somersault. I was really worried about Jay and turned the boat around quickly. I expected him to be hurt, but he was laughing and said, "That was really fun!" He never did get back into the tube again, though. To this day I have this picture in my mind of Jay Osmond rolling over backwards like he was in slow motion as we saw his feet up over his head.

—Rob Harris (My Brother-in-Law)

I still remember this particular time we went to Rob's parents' house for dinner. I still couldn't speak English at this point. Jay and Kandi were there, and Jay welcomed me by saying, "Hola!" I responded with the little bit of English I knew, and he was so patient with me. Jay really made me feel comfortable. I'm impressed how Jay always appears to be happy and have a smile on his face. That is a gift from God. I think Jay inspires a lot of people with his personality, because even though life can be hard, he reminds people how important it is to give the little gift of a smile. He is also a wonderful father. I thank Jay for being such a good example as a father, and as a friend.

—Luz Harris (Rob's wife, my Sister-in-Law)

Travis and Keri

When I think about Travis and Keri, I remember a funny thing that happened when they were first married. We were at the annual Harris Family Reunion in Portage, Utah. Travis and Keri are both very adventurous and have camped a lot. Our kids were little, and we had decided we would stay in a tent that year (rather than a motel or motor home). Neither Kandi nor I really enjoy camping, but we chose to do it that year in order to be with her family—and because we thought it would be a good experience for our boys. Travis and Keri's tent was pitched just a few feet from ours, and when it became dark, we all went into our tents for the night. Kandi, the boys, and I knelt down for family prayer, and we forgot that others could hear us. As I said the prayer, I asked Heavenly Father to help us have a good tenting experience. We'll never forget the muffled laughter we heard coming from Travis and Keri's tent.

>   *One of my favorite memories of Jay occurred years ago after a day of fishing with Jay, Jason, and Eric at Deer Creek Reservoir. We had hiked along the lake shore and fished all morning—where Jason and Eric had more fun sliding down the dirt bank like a slippery slide than they did fishing. We then drove down Provo Canyon to a fast food restaurant for lunch. We had just pulled in and were walking toward the front sidewalk of the place when, all of a sudden, a truck raced into the parking lot with the radio blasting super loud and whipped into the parking space right in front of our group on the sidewalk. Two rough-looking guys wearing greasy mechanic coveralls jumped out of their vehicle and, to their great surprise (and mine), were immediately confronted by Jay Osmond—a papa bear with cubs. Jay forcefully told them that he did not appreciate the way they had pulled into the parking lot and told them to slow down because there were kids present. Although the two grease monkeys looked quite surprised and were left seething, both knew they were in the wrong, and neither one of them dared utter a word of defiance. In the end, I think their biggest surprise came not from the unexpected enforcement of their reckless driving, but rather, from being called of all things, "A couple of turkeys!"*
>
>   *—Travis Harris (My Brother-in-Law)*
>
>   *I'll never forget something Jay said at Marcus's 5th birthday party (at their condo in Provo). Marcus had recently gone along on one of Jay's performing cruises. We got to talking about cruises and how much fun one would be—which sounded like a dream vacation to us.*

Jay shared his view on cruises by saying that cruises are not very much fun to go on because all they consist of is swimming pools, buffets, and beaches. The whole room went silent, and then Jay burst out laughing once he saw our incredulous faces staring in disbelief. It turns out there is a big difference between a vacation cruise and a working cruise—where relaxation and anonymity are anything but ordinary.

—*Keri Harris (Travis's wife, my Sister-in-Law)*

Kevin and Sharee

Kevin and his family have recently moved out-of-state but used to live not too far away from us, so we've seen them often. Kevin is a fun guy and is really creative. Kandi has had so much fun working with her brother and his wife, Sharee, when they opened up "Kandi's Korner" with her. Kevin is around the age of some of our boys' cousins, so he has sort of felt more like a cousin to them. We'll miss having them live nearby.

One of my first memories of Jay was of him at our house in California during some kind of get together with a lot of people. I remember him announcing that he needed a hair from a woman's head and one from a man's head to demonstrate something he had recently learned. He claimed that if the two hairs were placed somewhat close together in some water they would react or "fight" with each other. He got two hairs and a glass of water. He poured a small puddle of water on the table and placed the two hairs next to each other. Everyone gathered around to see if this actually worked. He added a little more water, but nothing was happening. He asked for more water and added that to it. "Look!" he said, suddenly pointing at the hairs. As we all leaned in, he slapped his hand down on the table, splashing everyone!

I remember staying at a hotel with Jay to help babysit Jason during a performance. In the morning, we went to the restaurant in the hotel for breakfast. I was surprised that Jay never even opened his menu. He just started asking the waiter if they had certain things and then telling him what he wanted. I specifically remember him asking for cantaloupe for Jason and describing to the waiter how he wanted it cut, etc. I showed the waiter a little mercy when I ordered something off the menu exactly as it was written.

After Jason was born, Jay would refer to me as "Uncle Kevin" so that Jason would know what to call me. Since I was more the age of one of Jason's cousins rather than an uncle, Jay ended up referring to me as "Uncle Kevin," "Kevin," and "Cousin Kevin." He always had to stop and think before getting it right. One day, Jay was in a hurry to get somewhere and said to Jason, "You are going with Kevin and Uncle Daddy." That was the best yet! I still sometimes call Jay, "Uncle Daddy."

—*Kevin Harris (My Brother-in-Law)*

While I was engaged to Kevin (Kandi's brother), I stayed at Jay and Kandi's house for a week. I was in my last semester of college with a full load of classes, working two part-time jobs, and getting ready for my upcoming wedding. The stress was taking its toll. Jay could see I was making myself sick, so he took the time to sit down with me and see if he could help. We talked about everything that was going on in my life. He made sure I was eating and sleeping, then helped me see what was most important at that moment in my life. He told me it was all right to let some things go. I don't remember all that was said that day, but I didn't feel so overwhelmed by life after our talk.

I was impressed by the amount of love and care I felt from this man I just recently met. At the time, it was amazing to me that with all he had to do, he could still find the time and energy to care about me. Jay has such a large heart. He easily loves and cares for those around him. This memory quickly became just one of many where he would say or do something to ease our family's burdens.

—Sharee Harris (Kevin's wife, my Sister-in-Law)

STAGE RIGHT OR STAGE LEFT?

After all of my years performing, I could never get this right. To me, stage right was on my right, but to a director, it is their right as they face the stage—or is it the opposite? This is an example of how we all have different perspectives for how we look at things. You've read how I've looked at things throughout my life. Now read how others have seen me. Following are stories as only these friends can tell them.

Bailing Out the Best Man

I've often been asked how it came to be that Jay asked me to be the best man at his wedding to Kandilyn. I've always responded by saying, "When you have eight brothers to pick a best man from, you go outside the family!" But, seriously, Jay and I became very good friends back when he was at BYU—and boy do I have stories from those days.

There was the time when Jay tried out for the BYU football team. At that time, I had finished playing football and was a student coach. Jay was one of my players during spring practice. When we weren't practicing football, we were meeting girls together on campus at BYU. We'd also go to Logan, Utah together, and he'd line me up with girls. There was the time Jay bought a Highball game, and we got into being the Highball champions of the area. (We were champions primarily because no one else had one of the game. Highball was a game of basketball played on a trampoline.) Jay had a flag football team when we first became really good friends. We ended up being ranked in the BYU polls for football teams and had a pretty good year and a fun experience. I also worked for the Osmond family when they had their studio in Utah.

The Osmond Brothers once came to Newport, California, where I lived, to perform. Jay called to invite me to go out for tacos after the show. We got into my old car (which had a taillight out that I forgot about) and set out to get some tacos. We were driving around and talking when I realized a police car had come up behind us. I was pulled over for the broken taillight, and the officer said he'd have to run my driver's license through a check. This is where it gets dicey! Four years earlier, I had a speeding ticket in Orange County that I never paid. I thought the time had run out on it, but the license check came back showing there was an outstanding warrant for my arrest. The policeman proceeded to handcuff me and said they'd have to take me to jail. I gave Jay the car keys, and he hurried back to his hotel, rounding up his brothers and taking a collection until he had the $161 in cash that was needed to bail me out of jail. Jay arrived at the jail to pay my bail and everyone there realized he was an Osmond—so they invited him on a tour of the jail facility. I couldn't believe that Jay got me out, but then I had to go on a special tour of the place with him. By the way, I wanted to pay the bail money back to Jay, but he wouldn't take it. This is one of many memories that show what a great person Jay is.

—Dave Smith (Best Man)

Jay, Football, and Emerson

I first met Jay in the football locker room at BYU. Jay was a quarterback and could really throw the ball. We found that we had two things in common: we liked to toss the football around, and we both liked looking for girls. Jay amazed me with his gifted approach to meeting a new girl. I marveled as he would walk up and say, "Excuse me, excuse me, what's your name?" Amazingly, the young lady would always answer.

Jay has an unquenchable thirst for knowledge. I was a brand-new member of the church and would ask Jay for answers to gospel questions. If Jay didn't know the answer, he seemed to always know where to find it.

Jay has a joke or one-liner for just about any situation; and if there isn't a situation, he'll create one just so he can make you laugh with one of the million funnies he has stored away in his noggin.

I think the thing that impresses me most about Jay is his commitment to be a great friend. Emerson once said, "A great friend is one whom you can't think of without elevation." Throughout my life and its many challenges, Jay has always been available to be a listening ear, and he always has words of encouragement and optimism to make one feel better.

—Bob Kittell (Motivational Speaker)

Jay's Real Self

The world is filled with towering walls of egos and defenses, pretenses and facades, all piled so high that it's easy to feel alone sometimes, even though we are here with six billion or so others. But, once in awhile, someone comes along like a star shining through a cloudy night and, with a big warm smile, gives something singularly wonderful to the entire world—himself, his real self. Jay is one of those people. When Jay is excited, we all know. When he is in pain, he shares that, too. His questions about life and love and everything else show up on his face like a story in a book—he is easy to read. He is easy to talk to and to share with, because he shares. He is easy to love, because he loves.

—John Canaan (Solo Artist)

Man of Destiny at 5:00 A.M.

I couldn't resist this opportunity to skewer Jay just a little with two stories that have always stuck with me:

Jay instructed me in the four-step "rise and shout" technique he developed over the years, so that he wouldn't be the last one in a limo. I remember one time when we were traveling, there was a mix-up and we were short on hotel rooms for the group—so Jay and I had to room together. Jay was sleeping soundly in the room we were sharing (Wayne must have made the travel arrangements on this one!) when Jay's alarm went off at 5:00 A.M. Most people throw an arm out blindly groping just to turn off the intrusion as quickly as possible. Not Jay. I opened one eye just soon enough to catch a flurry of blankets flying; a lightning fast sit-up; and Jay's legs swinging to the side of the bed, then onto the floor. With one quick motion he was on his feet smiling—a man of destiny ready for the new day. This was long before reminder tools such as Franklin Quest or the Covey Institute. Jay has always been an innovator— this technique has allowed him through all these years to be just a step ahead of the rest of humanity.

I also remember Herb Alpert looking at Jay with surprise and wonder as Jay played drums in a video shoot for Herb's wife, Lani. He had no idea that Jay could *really* play.

—*Sam Cardon (Songwriter/Artist)*

Disco Diva and Matchmaker

Jay and I first met when he was doing a *Learn to Disco Dance with Jay Osmond* video. He produced it at the disco I owned with my brother: the Star Palace in Provo, Utah. It was the largest disco in the nation at the time (Wolfman Jack was our DJ), and it was a fun place that Jay liked to visit. Over time, Jay and I became the best of friends, and he even asked me to be roommates with Jimmy and him.

George Osmond (we called him "King George") taught us that "your home is your castle" and a person should be very selective about who they let into their private life. So, I was honored when he'd tell me I was one of his boys and that I was always welcome in their home. George was the head of the home and Olive was the heart of the home, but they walked side by side as they made decisions together. They were such good examples.

Out of all the Osmonds, Jay and I had the most in common and were closest in age. We'd often compare notes from our journals about what we thought were the most important qualities in the girls we each would like to marry.

My brother and I had another one of our Star Palace discos in Rexburg, Idaho; and on one of my business trips there, I met a wonderful girl. Stephanie was the most popular girl on campus at Ricks College—a happy, positive, assertive, beautiful girl—and I fell in love from the start.

In 1983, the Osmond family went to Rexburg, Idaho to do a concert at Ricks College (in those days, I traveled with the Osmond Brothers). I told Jay that I wanted to see this girl again, so he said he'd get a date and we would bring the girls as guests to the concert. When I went to pick Stephanie up for the show, I found she had stood me up. Jay was with me, and he was so distraught about this. I remember him saying, "Braddy, I feel so bad, she shouldn't have done that!"

Jay just couldn't let it go and, two weeks later, told me he had an idea. Even though Stephanie stood me up and broke my heart, Jay knew there was something special about this girl for me. He said that she just didn't know me and he was going to fix it. Jay's plan was for us to drive to Rexburg in my Corvette. We were going to meet some girls, show them the time of their lives, and make Stephanie jealous. We did, and we had a wonderful time. My date was one of the college's cheerleaders, and she seemed to really like me. According to Jay's plan, Stephanie heard about it.

After we "painted the town red," we both had to get back home; so we left late at night to make the drive home to Provo. The heater in my Corvette quit working and it was the middle of winter. We put the extra clothes we had with us over what we were already wearing, along with jackets, blankets, and anything else we could put on to stay warm. We made the five-hour drive in sub-zero temperatures. We nearly froze to death but talked all the way back. Jay said Stephanie would hear that this other girl wanted to go out with me again and assured me that we accomplished what he wanted to do for me—make Stephanie jealous. He said to just give her time; he counseled me like a brother with love and respect and reminded me I had a feeling about her that I shouldn't dismiss.

To make a long story short, Stephanie and I became engaged and got married. We look to Jay to this day as our hero for taking the time to search out something that was inevitable, but probably wouldn't have come together without his wisdom and unique unselfishness. We'll be forever grateful for his part in bringing us together and for his unselfish friendship. We have children who are outstanding, bright, sensitive, and smart—and it is because of whom I married. None of these people would be in my life if it weren't for my dear friend Jay Osmond.

To have a friend you have to really be a friend, and I learned that from Jay.

—*Brad Weekes (Real Estate Developer)*

Early Social Networking

In the mid 1970s, life for the Osmond family was anything but normal, as most of us know life. Jay was heavily involved in live concert performances, recordings, rehearsals, production, a variety show, and countless community and professional appearances. This left little time for him to engage in many of the normal teenage activities centered in school, such as proms, athletic events and dating.

I first met Jay, Donny, and Marie when I moved to Provo, Utah in February 1974. We attended the same LDS ward and quickly became friends. I believe it was due to the fact that we had a mutual respect for one another and treated each other as true friends, looking past and setting aside their professional status.

With his busy schedule, what free time Jay had was precious to him and, as normal to teenage boys, girls and dating were a high priority. My assignment, if I may refer to it as such, was to help Jay and Donny get lined up with dates when they were in town and had some free time. We talked a lot on the phone when they were on the road so we could coordinate their schedule. I would, on occasion, be able to take photos of different young women that I thought they would be interested in. I had a fairly good picture of the type and personalities that Jay liked, and my attendance at Provo High School gave me a pool of young ladies to draw from.

Depending on the situation, I would either set up the date or give Jay the girl's phone number (asking for her permission prior to giving it out), and he would call them. There were a few girls who refused to give me their numbers and said that they were not interested, but I never told Jay about those as I didn't want to hurt his feelings. We would generally double date.

The dates were pretty typical for those days. A movie, bowling, eating at a local burger joint, and dancing at the local dance hall were all very common. If there was a concert coming to the area with another performing artist, we would generally try to attend and always ended up with backstage passes and a chance to meet the artists. This would always be a thrill for Jay's date. One of our favorite places to end up was The Ice House, a local dance hall. Jay loved to dance and show off his moves on the floor. Let's face it: he had a lot of rehearsal time and talent in this area, besides his percussion and vocal abilities. The music at the dance hall was mostly live; and one local band, Copperfield, would invite Jay up to accompany them on a few songs.

I remember one young lady that I was trying to line Jay up with. Her name was Debbie. I can't remember if it was before or after she went out on a date with Jay, but she made it very clear to me that she was more interested in going out with Donny. Debbie did end up with Donny . . . and is his wife today.

Jay's free time was not just about dating. We spent a lot of time just sitting around the house, talking, goofing off, playing games, watching movies, and discussing the differences in our lifestyles. I often thought how neat it would be to go on stage and perform in front of a large audience of screaming fans; and Jay often thought how neat it would be to go to school on a regular basis and attend school activities such as pep rallies, basketball games, dances, and such.

In due time, I left on my LDS mission. Jay attended my farewell meeting and also saw me off at the airport. We stayed in touch throughout my mission. He always felt that he missed out on not being able to be a full-time missionary for two years, preaching the gospel to the people. I reminded him that through his professional career and example, he touched more lives and brought the message of the gospel to more people than I ever dreamed of touching.

The Osmonds did perform in the mission area where I was serving. Jay called my mission president to see if he could meet with me. With the president's permission and a few logistics, I was able to spend time with them before their performance. I took my mission companion with me, and he was amazed at all that had to come together for a performance. Jay and I spent some time just catching up and talking about what we had been doing. He was most anxious to hear about those that had been converted and other experiences I had on my mission. It was good to see him.

After my two-year mission, Jay was there to greet me at the airport upon my arrival home. It's great to have true friends in this world, and I have been blessed to have Jay as one of mine.

Jay and I still stay in touch, though not as often as we'd like. We still see each other on special occasions, but it seems that the rigors of our individual family life and our personal professions consume the majority of our time.

—*Charles T. Wixom (High School Friend)*

Defending the Family

Anybody who has been around Jay for any period of time knows his crazy, fun-loving side. That's pretty much the real Jay—crazy, fun-loving, genuine, kind, and sincere, with a dash of absent-mindedness (a trait we happen to share). Unless you've seen him perform, you would have no clue he is a world-class drummer. Anyone as unassuming and humble as Jay couldn't possess that kind of talent. But he does. Even after seeing him perform so many times, I'm still blown away whenever I see him get behind the drums.

There's another side of Jay that I recall seeing only once—about 25 years ago. During his single days, Jay was known to have dated quite a bit. Okay, that's an understatement. The propensity to flirt was something else the two of us had in common, although I don't know that I was ever in Jay's league in that department.

One evening we were at Sundance (Utah) for some reason. I didn't think anything of it when I turned around in the parking lot and Jay was socializing with a couple of young ladies. Naturally I approached to join in. What neither one of us knew was that these girls had come to Sundance with a couple of guys (being oblivious to that kind of detail is one more tendency Jay and I share). It turned out the two guys were members of the BYU Football Team, and they weren't happy. I don't think Jay would have knowingly stepped on these guys' toes—whether or not they were bigger than he was. It's not in Jay's nature to cause trouble, but he inadvertently did, and some words were said. I didn't hear everything, but what stands out in my memory to this day was Jay's defiance when he heard an insulting comment about his family. He said something like, "You can say what you want about me, but when I hear my family being bad-mouthed, it makes my blood boil!" He said it with such confidence and strength and righteous indignation that I didn't hear another peep from the two guys. We all could see that his blood was boiling. I remember thinking, "I can't believe this is my buddy Jay! Where did that side of him come from?" But, that's Jay. He has a fire in his belly when it's called for. He is one of the most technically amazing drummers around and has entertained millions all over the world; yet, he is genuine, meek, and down-to-earth.

—*Chris Coburn (Fellow Former Flirt)*

Smiling from Day One

I remember Jay as a bright, smiling infant who wanted to get on with life. I think he had the feeling that he didn't want to be hampered with an infant's body any longer than was absolutely necessary. This proved to be true later as Jay excelled in all the many things that came into his life.

Jay was really cute as the youngest member of the group on *The Andy Williams Show* with those two front teeth missing. It was fun watching him perform. His grandparents thought he was a great part of the act, too. In fact, he was the heartthrob of a great many of the older generation!

Jay has always been happy and enthusiastic. I guess this comes from his wanting to get on with life from the time he was a baby. This has rubbed off onto others, making others' lives a little more happy and upbeat than they were before meeting Jay.

When we lived in St. George, Utah, we used to enjoy visiting the Osmonds in California or Las Vegas. We were always greeted by Jay with that happy smile and, "How are you Uncle Tom and Aunt Helene?" It was this kind of reception that just made us melt on many occasions.

Much later, I had a teaching position at the College of Eastern Utah, and Jay would always track me down to say hello. He still gave that familiar warm reception to his old uncle. Looking back on Jay's life, I can understand why he was so good at the job he had with BYU. He was good because he excelled with public relations; and he was good with public relations because of the good feelings people get from being around him.

—*Tom and Helene Davis (Uncle and Aunt)*

What's in the Suitcase?

One of my wife Melanie's favorite "Jay moments" was the time he came to Los Angeles to stay with us. Upon his arrival, he opened his suitcase to show me some papers. Instead, out fell an apple, an avocado, and his underwear!

—*John Edmunds (Attorney)*

Double Dating with Thelma and Marie

I fondly remember the time when Jay and I took "Thelma," the CPR/Artificial Resuscitation Training Dummy, out on the town. We tied her to the luggage rack on top of my car and drove around. When we pulled up to a gas station, the attendant came out and asked, "Can I help you?" We replied, "Yes, we're looking for our mother." We then took her to a popular pizza restaurant where Marie was on a date. We all sat down (including Thelma) in the same booth with Marie and her date. Everybody in the restaurant had a good laugh.

Then there was the time we were performing in Pittsburgh, Pennsylvania. We had a night off, so we went to see a movie. Alan, Wayne, and I bought Jay a bag of popcorn just so we could see him walk down the aisle, deliberately trip and fall, and toss popcorn into the air (a joke I'm pleased to say he learned from me).

Of course, who can forget the day Jay boarded the tour bus with what he said were sugarless cookies. After we all started eating them, he announced they were actually dog biscuits.

And one of my favorite memories was when we were in Hong Kong hiking up a scenic trail that overlooked Mainland China. Ron Clark was on crutches with a broken ankle, so Jay and Donny offered to help him walk with us. Then, they took away his crutches and left him standing there as they said, "See ya later, Ron!" (They came right back, though!)

—*Walt Gregory (Keyboard Player)*

Jay Gets Busted

A memory of Jay that stands out for me was during *The Osmond Family Christmas Special,* the most popular show of the year (and, for me, the most stressful). I handled tickets for shows at the studio, and I became very popular during showtime. A lot of requests were coming my way, including one from Jay. I put him down for four tickets. The night of the taping, he asked me to take care of his friends. I often took care of special guests and didn't give it much thought. When it was almost time to seat Jay's friends, he informed me that his friends were actually four girls that he was dating. He wanted me to seat them in different places in the audience. I guess I was stressed enough that his request pushed me over the edge. I didn't have time to take care of his girlfriends, individually, so I had them all sit in the front row next to the stage and next to each other. When Jay and his brothers came on stage to perform, he saw what I had done, and he was not happy with me. He called me to the stage during a break and asked me what I was thinking, but he was powerless to do anything. That old saying is really true. The show must go on—even if your girlfriends are sitting on the front row getting acquainted with each other.

—*Cindy Wankier Clark (Tour Manager)*

Where Did You Put That Gum?

This is a classic "Jay story" that Norm Finlinson loved to tell. Norm was BYU's Director of Admissions at the time. Norm invited Jay to a BYU football game; and of course, Jay accepted the invitation. Their seats, however, happened to be located directly beneath one of the loudspeakers, causing Jay great pain. Jay has a sensitivity of the ears as a result from the loudness of performing on stage. Trying to alleviate the pain without bringing too much attention to himself, Jay used the only thing he could find to use as earplugs—chewing gum. Evidently, Jay had to push the gum in quite far before experiencing relief, but he was able to do so and went on to enjoy the rest of the game. After the game was over, and after he and Norm departed, Jay went to remove the gum from his ears, only to find that he had pushed it in so far, he couldn't get it out. Jay ended up in the emergency room at the hospital to have the gum surgically removed. One of the funniest parts of this story is that Jay went to work the next day and told us all about it!

—*Raylene Hadley (Colleague from BYU and Friend)*

Christmas Eve and Raccoon Eyes

When I think about Jay, there are two words that come to my mind: joy and laughter. Joy, because Jay has a humble heart and truly desires to serve others. This was shown to me over and over by the way Jay makes sure everyone else is okay. Jay is always concerned about others and tries to ease their burdens by bringing joy to their lives. He continually does this on many occasions—anonymously. I will always remember how, even though I was the "outsider looking in" working for Jay, I was continually impressed by his continued goal of serving the Lord by serving others, and by the humble way he went about it.

The stories I'm sharing are from around 1983–87. One Christmas Eve, Jay, Jimmy, myself, and a couple of other friends went to share some joy with others by delivering a Christmas tree, food, and gifts to a couple of families in the area who were unable to have much for Christmas on their own. We loaded everything up that evening into his father's old pickup truck, and we all piled into the front and headed on our way to deliver the gifts anonymously. We snuck up to the doorsteps of those homes then rang the doorbell before we ran back to the truck across the street and hid behind it. The joy I felt from being able to serve others was so humbling, to this day I still get a little choked up when I talk about it. My family was away in another state at the time, so the experience especially touched me. Those memories are among those I still cherish. I will never forget the feeling I had as we drove back to Jay's mother and father's home, singing Christmas carols all the way. Both Jay and Jimmy taught me about the gift of giving anonymously that evening, and I still strive to continue spreading that joy.

When Jay made the decision to work at Brigham Young University, I remember that transition very clearly. He went from being a performer to a Monday-through-Friday employee. He felt like he had been a boy inside a bubble, and he was experiencing the opportunity to burst that bubble and begin a "normal life." I found that interesting from Jay's perspective, because it took me a long time to understand that his "normal" was so different from mine.

To be able to watch and observe Jay through that transition, and observe the integrity and honesty he showed, is still with me to this day, even though so many years have gone by. I believe it was one of the decisions in his life which truly brought forth the incredible man he has become today. In fact, if Jay had not made the decision to work at BYU, maybe he wouldn't have met his wife, Kandilyn. Kandi was definitely the person that Jay was meant to spend his life with. She has a warm heart, is a loving mother, and lives the gospel. Jay could not have done better. That was the reason it took him so long to get married. The timing of him going to work at BYU, and Kandilyn showing up at the admissions office to get an application for her brother, was no mere coincidence.

I don't think I taught Jay much while I worked with him (although trying to be more organized may be one thing), but he made me laugh all the time. The things Jay came up with and did were hysterically funny most of the time. I remember one particular instance when Jay decided he wanted to use a suntan bed. One of our friends owned the suntan salon in Provo, Utah, so I called him up and scheduled an appointment for Jay. I remember telling Jay that the first couple of visits to tan needed to be limited in time. I clearly told him ten minutes or so ought to be good. Jay went with good intention, but said he fell asleep and ended up staying in for 30 minutes. We laughed for hours over his raccoon eyes that afternoon. Later that evening, I received a call from a frantic Jay; he was almost hyperventilating because he was in so much pain. I picked him up and raced to the local drug store to get some Solarcaine for the burn. He was screaming when he sprayed it on his arms and legs. I was laughing so hard I had tears in my eyes. I still laugh even while sharing this, because to this day it was one of the most hysterical moments I have experienced with him.

The funniest thing about these stories is that Jay is such a great storyteller; when he would share these life experiences, he would laugh just as much as everyone else. We'd always find ourselves laughing until our sides hurt.

Those are just a couple of my memories of Jay. I can't believe so many years have gone by since those experiences. They are in my heart and mind as if they just happened yesterday. I do know that the opportunity I had to work with Jay and his family is one I wouldn't trade for anything. Jay holds a special place in my heart, and the memories of those times have truly brought me joy and laughter throughout my life. Even though our lives have taken us on separate journeys, he is a true friend and will always hold a special place in my heart. Thanks Jay, for allowing me to share those times with you. I will never forget what you have taught me.

—*Linda Neeley (Secretary and Wedding Planner)*

The Famous Grin

As Jay was growing up in Ogden, we would often visit the family. We watched Jay grow from a very small baby to a wonderful man. When they were with Andy Williams, we loved to see Jay "steal the show" with that famous grin as he followed the camera. Many of our friends would talk about that. Jay always comes up with a nickname for everyone. He called a lot of us "turkey," which fit in some cases. Jay is a very special spirit; Heavenly Father sends at least one of those to every family.

—*Rulon and Norma Osmond (Uncle and Aunt)*

Second Chances?

One incident I cherish the memory of occurred in the foyer of the ASB at Brigham Young University. Jay and I were discussing the mysteries of life, when a very attractive young lady entered from the south wing. Jay pointed her out to me and hinted that he might ask her out. The next thing I knew, Jay approached her and began his polished approach. She seemed receptive, at least for the first few seconds; then she interrupted by saying, "Jay, we've already gone out!" To which he responded, "I'm sorry, what was your name . . . and would you like to go out again?"

—*J. Rex Pugmire (BYU Colleague)*

Apricots and Driving Don't Mix

One time, Jay and I were driving from Denver to a meeting in Colorado Springs with a group of colleagues. We were about halfway there when Jay spoke up, "Derek, can we go back? I left my day planner on the front desk at the hotel when I stopped to get an apple, and it has our directions in it. Sorry!"

Another funny memory is about Jay's love for apricots. Carol knew Jay loved them, so she picked a small bucket and gave them to him prior to a trip we were taking to Idaho. We thought the four of us in the car could enjoy them during the drive but soon realized Jay had eaten them all before we reached the freeway entrance. Thank goodness for rest stops.

—Derek and Carol Spriggs (BYU Colleagues)

Showering with Socks

Tom Gourley, Norm Finlinson, Jay, and I used to play racquetball during our lunch hour. On one occasion, after a rousing game, we all retired to the showers, sweaty and exhausted. Jay always undressed a little more slowly than the rest of us, so it wasn't unusual for Tom, Norm, and me to get to the showers before Jay. The three of us were showering when Jay walked in, put his towel on the towel bar, grabbed his soap, and started to shower. Norm looked at Tom and me with a funny expression, then looked at Jay and said, "Jay, do you always shower with your socks on?" Jay was completely unaware he had forgotten to take off his socks.

—Kirk Strong (BYU Colleague)

Please Have a Popsicle!

As I think back on all the times we shared together, there is one memory that stands out above all the rest. It was the time Jay joined us on our trip to Ricks College in Rexburg, Idaho. On the way home, we stopped at a store, and we all went in to buy a few things. We waited and waited for Jay; no one knew where he was. Finally, he came out with a sack of groceries. We started down the road, and Jay began to enjoy a Popsicle. He asked if anyone else wanted one, and everyone said no. Jay looked concerned. A little later, he began to plead for people to have a Popsicle. It was then that we realized he had purchased a whole package of them, and they were becoming very, very soft. We all pitched in to help Jay out of his dilemma, only to find that he had purchased a lot of other food items he proceeded to consume on the way home. The most memorable were the apricots. As I recall, Jay called in sick the next day, which gave us all a good chuckle.

—*Jeff Tanner (BYU Supervisor)*

Green Thumb?

I never had the opportunity to actually work with Jay, but I know him from "the legend of Jay." There was a potted plant in my office that used to be in Jay's office. I was told that he watered it faithfully. I made sure to let Jay know I took good care of his plant after he left BYU—the plastic leaves remained shiny and bright. The fake Spanish moss did finally recover from being waterlogged and returned to its green and spongy texture. I suspect the plant will be around for a long, long time.

—*Marie Tueller (BYU Colleague)*

Where Do the Bullets Go?

One of my fondest memories of Jay is when we went target shooting on the west side of Utah Lake. We would usually meet early on Saturday morning, drive up the I–15, and get off at the Lehi exit to stop at the Circle K for a drink and donuts. After this pit stop, we would head west to Redwood Road until we got to our shooting spot. Jay was always excited about this activity and always wanted to hold the cans while I was shooting. Many times I had to explain to Jay that this procedure would not work very well when I was using a 12-gauge shotgun. I remember clearly one morning when Jay spent nearly 20 minutes trying to load a semi-automatic pistol. I was wondering what was going on, because I hadn't heard any shots coming from where he was standing. He finally came to me in desperation and said, "George, can you come over here for a minute?" Upon checking the situation, I could see he was trying to put the wrong type of ammunition into the pistol. We had a good laugh after that; and from that day on, I asked Jay to shoot in the next canyon over from me. He was always good about respecting my wishes after that.

—*George Vaieland (BYU Head Counselor)*

Don't Use the Shower!

My favorite "Jay story" is the time on tour in Des Moines, Iowa, when I was serving as the road manager for the group. I was checking everyone in to the local Holiday Inn. We arrived earlier than expected, so the rooms weren't ready for us, yet. Jay was really tired and said, "Hey Brother Bill, please get my room first. I really need to take a nap." I asked the hotel clerk for Jay's key, and he informed both of us that he would give us the key to a temporary room if Jay promised not to use the bathtub. There was a problem with the tub's drain, and the plumber hadn't finished the repair work. Jay said, "Oh, don't worry; I am going right to sleep!"

It wasn't five minutes later when water began cascading down from the ceiling tiles onto the hotel clerk's head and desk. Jay went right to the room and jumped into the shower.

—*Bill Waite (Donny's Former Manager)*

Plant Stealer

I worked with Jay at BYU. I had a plant on my desk that wasn't doing well. Jay's office had direct sunlight, so I asked him if he would keep it for a few days to see if that helped. A few days later, his secretary was out sick. Later that afternoon, I saw my plant on her desk with a note attached. Curious as to what it was doing there, I read the note. Jay was wishing her well and giving her my plant to brighten her day. Needless to say, everyone thought I should tell Jay he was giving away my plant. I didn't want to embarrass him, so I let it go. Someone in the office told Jay, though; and a couple days of later, a huge azalea plant appeared on my desk with an apology.

—*Patty Williams (BYU Admissions Officer)*

Where Are We Now?

Some of the special memories I have of my friendship with Jay have had quite an impact on my life. Without Jay, I would never have been introduced to frozen peanut butter sandwiches. I sleep better at nights because of the tape he sent to me on how to relax and get to sleep. I could never forget the phone calls I used to get from Jay when he was on the road performing. I would ask Jay where he was calling from, and he would pause to ask one of his brothers!

—*Bill Jenson (Delta Airlines Representative)*

A Gracious (Green) Date

Cole-Waite Enterprises, meaning Chris Cole and Bill Waite, was created in 1975 when we acquired the contract to do the concert merchandising for the Osmonds. At the time, we were both law students in Orange County, California. That contract led to many adventures and a bond of friendship now well into its fourth decade. Jay played a key role in our connecting with the Osmonds, which is a story in itself.

At Brigham Young University, I had the good fortune to date a beautiful young lady who happened to be the older sister of the girl that Donny Osmond would one day marry. Even after graduation I would still see Pam Glenn from time to time, as Bill and I would return to Provo, Utah to ski and chase college girls during breaks from law school. It was during Christmas break in 1975 when we knocked on the door of the Osmond home with hopeful hearts of presenting our business proposal. We met the family patriarch, George Osmond, and made our pitch. At the time, *The Donny & Marie Show* pilot had been picked up and the family was preparing to move the entire clan to Southern California. George invited us to come see them in Los Angeles after the holidays.

Pam Glenn not only attended school in Provo, but she also lived there with her family. On this same trip, I had occasion to visit the Glenn household, where I explained to Pam, her mother, and her younger sister (the future Mrs. Donny Osmond) our plans to do a deal with the Osmonds in L. A. Since Debbie and Donny had already dated a few times, Pam and her mom insisted that I take one of Debbie's recent high school pictures to Donny.

About a week later, a couple of overdressed young men in three-piece suits presented themselves at the guard gate of the studio on Sunset Boulevard, where *The Donny & Marie Show* was being taped. When Bill and I announced we were there to meet with the Osmonds, we got that "yeah, right!" attitude from the guard. So, we waited while notice of our presence worked its way to the Osmonds. Eventually we saw a bicycle heading our way with Jay at the controls; he had been dispatched to see who we were. After a quick introduction, I pulled Debbie's picture from my pocket, which Jay immediately recognized. After that, it was all open arms, and we were escorted into the studio to meet the entire family. Thus, Jay was a central character in opening the door of opportunity with the family. That deal with the Osmonds led to contracts with other acts that enabled us to finance law school without further bank loans.

Since the eligible brothers, Jay and Donny, had little if any opportunity to meet eligible ladies to date in California, Bill and I used our connections (such as they were) to set up group dates for the four of us. Occasionally we would line up a date for Marie, as well. We had great fun during those days in the mid-1970s.

I recall one particular date where Jay gave us a good laugh. As a group, we went to Knott's Berry Farm, and Jay's date was a beautiful girl named Julie Dokos. Jay and I, along with our dates, went on the parachute ride together. This was a metal basket that lifted very high in the air, suspended for a moment, and then released without warning. The initial fall was intended, and with pretty effective results, to create a rush of anxiety. We each had our hands on the handrail of the basket as we ascended to the top. Somehow, Julie timed it exactly right—at the very second the basket released, she pulled Jay's hands from the handrail, and he felt the initial drop without the benefit of holding onto anything.

He screamed and turned a couple shades of green. Of course, once the shock wore off (about halfway to the bottom), his good humor kicked in and he enjoyed the gag with the rest of us.

One other group date comes to mind. We were all in Bill's truck with a camper that had one of those crawl-through windows to the cab. We were somewhere in Hollywood; the actual event I do not recall. When the evening concluded, we dropped Jay and Donny at their car in a nearby parking lot. However, a group of young kids had previously spotted us at a restaurant and followed us. The problem was they did not notice the part about Jay and Donny switching cars; so as Bill, myself, and the four ladies headed south, this car full of kids followed us the entire 50 miles to Orange County in hopes of meeting some famous people. They seemed to be nice kids. I wished we could have introduced them to Jay and Donny before they drove all the way back to Los Angeles.

The last thought I will share is about the thousands of fans and the regard in which their Osmond idols held them. Fans came in every size, shape, and attitude. I will say as a first-hand observer that the Osmonds, Jay included, were the most respectful and grateful celebrities anyone could imagine. It was a thrill and an honor to be a part of the Osmonds during those unforgettable years. And now, instead of talking about dates and flag football, Jay and I talk about our grown children, with an occasional recollection of those days long past.

—*Christopher A. Cole (Former Business Associate)*

He Is Old

I have been debating as to which story to tell about Jay. There are so many of them that I don't know where to begin!

Do I tell the story of when I first met Jay at Utah State University? Would Jay even remember the day we played against each other in the Homecoming Mud Bowl football game? Would he remember playing quarterback in his nice, clean, blue, matching jogging suit with a bright, white, clean towel tucked in the front to wipe his hands on? Would Jay remember the guy (me) that took his towel, wiped his muddy face and hands on it, then threw it back at him? Probably not. He is old.

Would Jay remember going with me on a double date with two beauty queens in Atlanta? Would he remember the private tour at the amusement park where we had the chance to pet the porpoises, ride the rollercoasters, and compete for stuffed animals for our dates? Would he remember me squirting him in the pants to embarrass him? Probably not. He is old.

Would he remember the tour of the aircraft testing center and meeting the test pilot, sitting in the cockpit, and visiting the flight simulator? Would he remember almost falling over when he lost his equilibrium during the flight simulation? Probably not. He is old.

Would he remember throwing Frisbees in the San Antonio Theater? Would he remember getting the Frisbee caught in one of the hanging chandeliers? Would he remember the theater management being very angry? Probably not. He is old.

Would he remember the drum solo in Las Vegas? Would he remember that as soon as the stage was dark except for the blinding spotlights centered on him, the entire band began to shoot spitwads at him while he was trying to play the drums? Probably not. He is old.

Would he remember the continuous drama of dating and all the advice I gave him during his dilemmas? Would he remember the point that all of the young women he dated were way out of his league? Especially the one he finally married? Probably not. He is old.

Would he remember getting even with the entire band by putting doggy treats in a brown bag and then telling the band they were health cookies and offering them to everyone? Probably. He is not that old.

The more I think about it, the more I realize there is only one way to sum up my association and friendship with Jay. I have been very fortunate to know him for over 25 years. He is a considerate, caring gentleman, and I am proud to say we are friends. I wish him all the best.

—Mike Williams (1980s Assistant Stage Manager)

My Little Brother

From the very moment I first met "my little brother," I was delighted with his energy and love of life. Everything around this character smacked with happiness and activity. He oozed with energy and verbal comments that made everyone laugh with (and at) him—something he enjoyed as much, if not more, than performing with the world's most published, promoted, and honored singing group.

Those were years of youth for all of us. We approached each and every new challenge and opportunity with drive and commitment. It was always exciting and difficult, but the journey was made easier by the antics of one Jay Osmond.

We became fast and lasting friends. I was committed to him—seeing that as many of the world's chores were off his shoulders as possible. He, in turn, committed to me his trust, his loyalty, his friendship, and even his confidence. That's what I continue to hold to this day—that confidence.

—Ron Clark (Publicist)

Stealing Jay's Thunder

Jay received a lot of attention as the "most eligible Osmond bachelor," usually in the form of waves, whistles, cookies, and gifts showered on him from the many eligible single women. I remember one occasion when Jay and I were walking through the Riviera Apartments (owned by the Osmond Family at the time). Some girls from the top balcony of an apartment whistled at Jay. Not to be outdone, I turned to the girls and yelled back, "Thank you!" I took away all of his thunder.

—De Von Tu'ua (Family Security)

Jay the Handyman

We, the Haynie family, don't know Jay Osmond the performer; we know Jay differently. To the children he is "Uncle Jay"; and to us, he is our friend. We cherish the friendship we have with Jay and his wonderful family.

When they first moved to Branson, Jay was such a paranoid dad. When Jason and Eric came over to play, he gave us detailed instructions to be with them at all times and not to ever let them out of our sight. The best part came with the first sleepover. Jay was on this safety kick, and he brought over six smoke alarms and was adamant that we install each of them. For our friend Jay, we put all six alarms up, even though we already had smoke alarms.

The final legendary story to share about Jay is when he wanted to learn to be a handyman. Dan Haynie cannot sing but can fix just about anything. Jay was determined to learn "the handyman skills" from Dan (as if those skills could be learned in one day). Dan was installing a bay window, and Jay came over early to learn and help. They worked all day ripping out the floor and putting in new supports and flooring. Finally, Jay was given the task of screwing in some of the boards. When he finished with one board he was so pleased—and even signed his handiwork right on the floor. Now we can forever say, "This is where Jay screwed up!" At the end of the day, we unanimously decided that Jay should not retire his voice. Those who sing just don't fix.

—*The Haynie Family (Dear Friends from Branson)*

The Taco Bell Home Teacher

Bishop Stephen L. Johnson called me into his office one day and asked me to home teach the Jay Osmond family. Jay and Kandilyn had just moved into our ward with their two sons, Jason and Eric. I very much enjoyed our home teaching visits and soon developed a great friendship with Jay. This was not an easy time for him.

Jay was trying to make the break from the entertainment world to a life away from the spotlight. It was not working too well. Jay was like a fish out of water. The stage was the only world he had ever known. It seemed like he was doing something different each time I visited. One month he was going to school, the next month he was involved in the hotel industry. The next month it was nothing. This uncertainty was having a negative effect, as stresses and strains crept into the family relationships. Jay and I would take our young sons to McDonalds, where they would play in the fun house balls while we talked. Jay would sometimes go out of town, and I would take him to the airport or pick him up when he returned. We spent a lot of time together, mostly with him talking and me listening. He was not happy. His life was so different now. He was not playing the drums. We couldn't even get him to sing in the ward choir. He was gaining weight and totally unaccustomed to the world he was now living in. The culture of the church even seemed to be foreign to him.

As a home teacher I felt very ineffective, and as a friend I felt very sad. During our association, I developed a brotherly love for Jay—not because he was a big star, but because I found him to be a very kind, friendly, and warm person. Yet, the difficulty within the family continued, and my concern for their welfare grew. Thinking I was still their home teacher and friend, I finally worked up enough courage to call Jay and ask if I could talk with him. We decided to have lunch, and he suggested that we meet at the Taco Bell near where he was living.

It was an emotional meeting. I listened while Jay told me of his sadness and confusion. I started to take over the conversation. I drilled him with direct questions about personal aspects of his life. He was willing to answer and seemed comfortable with my line of questioning. I probed into past experiences and feelings. I reached into future hopes and wishes. I was kind, but firm. During my questioning, how to help Jay finally came to me. He told me he felt kind of badly because he never served a full-time mission. I then sat up and said to him, "Jay, is it true that your performing career was considered to be your mission?" He said, "Yes." I said, "Is it true that you and your family members were set apart and designated as missionaries?" He again answered, "Yes." I then said boldly, "Have you ever been released?" He was quite subdued as he said, "No." I continued by saying, "Then what are you doing? If you haven't been released, then you had better get back to it."

He was shocked. I was shocked. I followed by saying, "This is your life. This is your mission. You were called to it, and you had better get to it until you are released."

We both just sat there speechless. It seemed so simple. This message was so clear. The Lord had spoken to us. We knew what to do. Jay reflected back on the counsel from President Harold B. Lee to the Osmonds as he warned them, "The family is being watched, and the church will be judged by many by what you do." President Lee's counsel continued with, "You'll be faced with much opposition. Always choose the option that will bring you closer to the Celestial Kingdom." I felt peace as I said, "Jay, stay connected to the church."

He arose from the table and sparkled as he said, "I need to go home to my family." Then, Jay smiled as he said, "I need to call my brothers. I need to go back to work, to my mission, to my life." That day in the Taco Bell, a life was changed, a family was saved, and the Lord's will was made known.

Jay returned home and found love and healing. He resumed his career and has been blessed for following his heart. I love Jay, and I am grateful to call him my friend. I claim no special position in this story, other than to acknowledge the inspiration of the Lord, as His will was made known to His son, Jay Osmond, that day. I do, however, smile with joy inside as Jay now affectionately refers to me as the "Taco Bell Home Teacher."

—*Charlie Rudd (Home Teacher)*

A Great Home Teacher

When I moved to Jay's neighborhood more than eight years ago, I knew I was getting a fantastic view of Mt. Timpanogos and

Mt. Mahogany, along with a very comfortable community. What I didn't expect was to gain a close friend who would influence my life and the hearts of my family. I knew that Jay was a very talented and incredible musician, singer, and performer; but I didn't know the depths of his heart and ability to love and serve others. He has been my backyard buddy and driveway assailant. It really doesn't matter if you see him; he will always get your attention (snowballs, soccer balls, or wild flying footballs).

For me, the best part of Jay is the way he loves my family. He has been our home teacher for many, many years and never fails to call on birthdays or send flowers for events. But what he does best is love them. He knows my family individually and prepares lessons specifically for us, not just what is convenient. He teaches of being well balanced with his "five-pointed star" (Mentally Positive, Physically Fit, Socially Aware, Spiritually Directed, and Financially Stable). He makes gospel principles reasonable and attainable. He is able to bring the love of the Savior into our home through his care and concern for us.

I love having a backstage pass to see the behind-the-scenes Jay. It is this Jay that loves his boys unconditionally and encourages them to find their groove without forcing them into his. I have watched him grow as a father as much as his boys have grown as young men. There have been two key ingredients to this growth: Humility—he knows that he can't do it on his own and is willing to admit to himself and his boys when he has been wrong or needs to back off; and a pure heart—no matter where he is in the world, he is thinking of his family and ways to be a better husband and father. He has entertained millions and performed for royalty and dignitaries, but I have never been more impressed by his actions than when he helps and serves his beautiful wife.

I have laughed, cried, and prayed with him; and each time I get a glimpse of a new layer of his heart. What you see on stage is not the entire package; the best part is the regular neighbor, friend, and home teacher.

It was once said that the true measure of a man is the stature of his friends. If that is true, I am a very lucky and fortunate man.

—*Blair Kent (Bishop)*

Object Lessons and Autographs

Jay has been our home teacher for about nine and a half years. He has been so great. Our kids, my husband, and I have just loved him. Jay always comes with a great object lesson directed towards the kids. I know the lessons have really stuck with them, because they aren't just boring dry lectures. The lessons always get them thinking and laughing. Every once in a while, they will bring up something Jay used in a lesson years ago, which shows what an impact he has made.

When our girls were younger, Donny was touring with the *Joseph and the Amazing Technicolor Dream Coat* production. Our girls loved both the play and Donny. Jay wasn't able to come to the girls' baptisms, so as a surprise he had Donny call them on their birthdays. When Donny called, he said, "Hi, this is Donny Osmond; my brother Jay asked me to call you to wish you a happy birthday!" Andie (our oldest) was so excited. I got off the phone and let her have her own conversation. He even sang to her, and this absolutely made her day.

Later, when Marissa turned eight, the girls wondered if Donny would be calling her, too. I told Marissa not to expect it or to ask for anything. On the day of her birthday, she ended up getting sick. I was busy vacuuming, and Marissa told me that someone had phoned. She was just too weak and sick to answer the phone when it rang, so I checked the message. It was a birthday greeting from Donny. She had had such a bad day: she had to leave school and all the fun there for her birthday; she couldn't have her birthday party; and now she missed a call from Donny. So I did something very bold. There was a number on the caller ID. I called it back and Donny answered. I told him how much I appreciated him calling Marissa and that she hadn't had a great birthday; I asked if he would talk to her. He was concerned and asked what happened, and I told him the story. He was more than happy to oblige. They talked for a while, and she instantly brightened up and had a big smile on her face.

Jay went out of his way to do something special to brighten my girls' birthdays, and I always have appreciated his kindness. That is just the way Jay is. He always checks up on us, always has a joke for us, and always calls us "silly." One day when he came to visit us, he became serious and said he had been to see his psychiatrist. I giggled a little and my husband gave me a look, but I knew one of Jay's jokes was coming.

When Jay turned 50, his sweet wife, Kandilyn, sent messages to all of Jay's friends, asking us to call or text Jay on his birthday (which I did). Since Jay had his brother call my girls on their birthdays, I thought it would be funny to have my brother call Jay on *his* birthday. He's nobody famous, but I still thought it would be funny. Our girls always say that they love the Osmonds and that their favorite is Jay.

Jay takes care of us in many different ways. He got Sabrina Bryan's autograph for them when he went to see Marie in *Dancing with the Stars*. They were very excited about that. Jay also knew my girls liked Miley Cyrus and let me know that he was going to try to get her autograph for them. One day Jay showed up at our door, asked for Marissa and Andie, and pulled out the signed pictures for them. The girls were so excited.

We have learned not to joke with the Osmonds about needing help. When we were still new to the area, our home's heater was giving us problems. I ran into Kandilyn at a church activity, and she asked how we were doing. Jay was out of town, and she wanted to know if there was anything she could do for us. I jokingly said, "Yes, you can come over and fix my heater." A few hours later, someone came to our home to find out about the heating problem. I asked if Jay Osmond had called them, and yes—he had. Jay just had to go the extra mile and make sure we were ok . . . even from Branson!

The first time Jay came to home teach us, he didn't have our phone number; so, he just showed up and introduced himself. My husband thought it was ironic that our home teacher would have a last name that is so well known in Utah. As we got to talking, Jay said something about moving from Missouri and things started to click in my husband's brain. He said, "Wait, you're *the* Jay Osmond?" We never expected this down-to-earth, friendly, caring, funny guy living in our neighborhood to be famous. Jay is still that way. He checks in on us, gives great lessons, makes us laugh, and helps us feel closer to the Lord. And we love him for it!

—*Carol Bailey (Neighbor)*

Who Is Dale Earnhart?

Jay and his brothers had a performance date in North Wilkesboro, North Carolina, not too far from where Terri and I live. We hadn't been living in North Carolina for long, so we were excited to have Jay come by our house the night before their concert. It was a beautiful evening, so we took Jay out for a boat ride. We sailed down the lake to a popular lakeside restaurant called, "The Rusty Rudder." We pulled into a boat slip, tied down the boat, and walked up the pier to the restaurant. We sat on the deck overlooking the lake and the sunset. Jay enjoyed a meal of his favorites—shrimp with orange juice to drink—and we had a great time. When we got back on the boat, Jay got out his cell phone and called his brother Jimmy. Jay said, "You wouldn't believe it, Jimper, we pulled the boat into a spot like you could park a car and went into the restaurant to eat!" Here was a guy who had travelled the world, and he found our little boating excursion fascinating. We got the biggest kick out of that.

As we pulled back into our own boat slip, we pointed out a house on the lake that belongs to one of our neighbors. We told him it was the home of Dale Earnhart's sister, and Jay asked, "Who is Dale Earnhart?" A dumbfounded Terri almost fell out of the boat, then teased Jay that he lives under a rock. Of all the places Jay has been, we find it amazing that he still talks about eating at the The Rusty Rudder on a lake in North Carolina.

—Jeff Shoemaker (Friend)

He Doubles as a Waiter

Jay and I were at the airport eating at a restaurant while we waited for our flight. A waitress dropped her tray; and without missing a beat in the conversation, Jay pulled out napkins, got down on his knees, and started mopping up the floor. The amazing thing was that he didn't even think twice about it; it came really naturally to him. Either he helps Kandi a lot with the housework, or Jay has done a little moonlighting as a waiter. Okay, so it could have also been a demonstration of what a good guy he is!

—Gaynor Brunson (Producer)

Hillbilly Cross-Dressers

My favorite memories of Jay always bring with them some great laughs. There was the boating trip we took on Table Rock Lake before one of the Osmond Brothers' shows in Branson. Wouldn't you know, the boat broke down. Jay had to paddle his heart out so he could get back in time for the show. With exhausted arms that were sure to challenge his big drum solo in the show, Jay made his way back to land and stage. Then there was the time Jay thought he'd be really funny and sent hillbilly cross-dressers to our store to sing happy birthday to me. Everyone was falling on the floor laughing. There is nothing Jay likes more than to see people having a good time with a lot of laughs. He never tires of making those things happen . . . oftentimes unintended.

—Robby Brusman (Former Stake President)

Camping Fun

One of my favorite stories comes from a time shortly after Jay and Kandi were married. It was nice to see them make the trip to Portage for the Harris Family Reunion. The moment they got out of the car, there was an unmistakable excitement in Jay. He was just like a Boy Scout going to his first summer camp. He enthusiastically pulled out their tent, though it appeared he didn't quite know how to set it up. As soon as the tent was standing, he was really quite excited to get inside to set up his sleeping bag and camping things. It was just fun to watch Jay, knowing that most of the camping he did growing up was in hotel rooms all over the world. That wasn't exactly the kind of camping he was about to embark on, though his energy and sense of anticipation made it fun for everyone.

—Dave DeLaMare (Kandi's Cousin)

Drum Battles with Dave

Uncle Jay and I have always shared a special bond as fellow drummers. I still remember my first drum lesson with Jay way back when I was just a kid. In fact, he was and continues to be one of my most influential drumming mentors. As I grew up and started my own drumming career, I realized just how incredibly talented he is. Jay's drum recordings in the 1970s were really groundbreaking pieces of work. He was playing some very progressive beats, and his style influenced a whole generation of up-and-coming drummers in the 1980s. Even now, the guy can flat-out play! Some of my favorite memories with Jay are the Christmas shows we did in Branson. We got to cut loose on the drums together in our rendition of "Little Drummer Boy." It was kind of a "drum battle" on stage; and frankly, Jay won every night!

—Dave Osmond (My Nephew and Virl's Son)

The Leftovers Are for the Raccoon

I remember the time I went to get into Jay's new car and noticed some kind of paw print on the hood. I asked Jay about it, and he responded with exasperation as he told me, "It's the raccoons around here—they climb into my car at night and eat the leftover McDonald's in my car!" Then he asked me, "Does that ever happen to you and Jimmy?"

—Michelle Osmond (Jimmy's wife)

My Uncle, Mr. Rogers

I remember when Uncle Jay would bring his dates over to our home and would have my brothers and me sing for them. I know we helped him score some serious points when we were kids. When he brought Aunt Kandi over on one of their dates, we sang her the song, "I Want Candy."

Uncle Jay went through a phase during the 1980s when he wore a lot of sweaters. We used to call him "Mr. Rogers." We were such nice kids!

When my brothers and I performed with our father and uncles at The Osmond Family Theater in Branson, Missouri, Jay always joked backstage that when he dies and goes to Heaven, he wants to have Kandilyn write on his tombstone, "He tried . . . he really tried!" Jay has a great sense of humor.

—Nathan Osmond (My Nephew and Alan's Son)

THE FINAL BOW

A t this point in my life, I find I'm starting to think about my own "refinement stage," as my father referred to it. I'm more open to doing projects on my own. I like the idea of creating some things that my sons can someday share with me and their own families. Unlike Donny and Marie, Jimmy, and Merrill, I've never had the desire to perform as a solo act, but I have learned I enjoy getting my hands into my own productions. In 1994, I released my first solo album which was a compilation of my favorite drum songs called, *It's About Time.* I thought about releasing a solo recording for 21 years and finally decided it was about time—which is obviously how the album's title came about. I released a solo CD of my rendition of "The Little Drummer Boy" during the Christmas season in 2008 and decided it was about time (again) to release a full-length solo CD. I selected my all-time favorite songs for this solo release and aptly gave it the title, *It's About Time Again.* My son Eric was the creative mind behind the project. I included a little synopsis for each song selection and reflected on my family as I did so. I was pleased with the outcome of the project, and the CD was released at the end of 2009.

About the same time I started working on *It's About Time Again,* I began to seriously work on this book. This book is another project that gave me the avenue to do a little something different on my own. Though I'm not a solo performer, I've become comfortable putting myself out there as just Jay Osmond—rather than always being part of a group.

When I know the time is right for me to take my final bow in show business, I'll perform one last show—and that particular show will be for *me*. It will be my closure to this wonderful, crazy, challenging world of show business. Looking out at the smiling faces in the audience has always given me a lift when I needed it—and during that show, I'll think about the stories behind their smiles and hope they know how important they have been in my life.

I'll also reflect on my amazing family and how we always come together when one of us is in need. It has been wonderful to be a part of this family, to work together for so many years and through so many challenges. It has been a great journey through life together, knowing we have had a purpose in being together. I'll wonder how many people can look back on their career and feel as richly blessed as I do.

The next stage will be a leap of faith for our whole family—to walk forward not knowing what is ahead, having faith in our abilities, each other, and most importantly in God.

INDEX